AN ARTS FOUNDATION COURSE

UNITS 10–12
INTRODUCTION TO ART HISTORY

Prepared by Erika Langmuir, Briony Fer and Linda Walsh
for the Course Team

The Open
University

Cover: *The Albert Memorial,* engraving by J. C. Armytage, from James Dafforne, *The Albert Memorial, Hyde Park: Its History and Description,* Virtue and Co., London, 1878.

The Open University, Walton Hall, Milton Keynes, MK7 6AA

First published 1986, third edition 1994

Copyright © 1986, 1994 The Open University

All rights reserved. No part of this publication may be reproduced, stored in a retrieval system or transmitted in any form or by any means without written permission from the publisher or without a licence from the Copyright Licensing Agency Ltd. Details of such licences (for photographic reproduction) may be obtained from the Copyright Licensing Agency Ltd of 90 Tottenham Court Road, London W1P 9HE.

Edited, designed and typeset by the Open University.

Printed in the United Kingdom by Page Bros, Norwich.

This text forms part of an Open University course. If you would like a copy of *Studying with the Open University,* please write to the Central Enquiry Service, PO Box 200, The Open University, Walton Hall, Milton Keynes, MK7 6YZ. If you have not already enrolled on the course and would like to buy this or other Open University material, please write to Open University Educational Enterprises Ltd, 12 Cofferidge Close, Stony Stratford, Milton Keynes MK11 1BY, United Kingdom.

ISBN 0 7492 2079 1

3.1

PREFACE: THE SEARCH FOR MEANING

The aim of these units is to acquaint you with the premises and methods of a special kind of history, the history of art. Yet there are many different kinds of art history, and the discipline is, as all others, constantly undergoing redefinition.

At the same time, of course, it is necessary to demonstrate something which may not be self-evident: that art is a human activity with a history; that is, an activity not unique to individuals and fresh-born with each practitioner, but a social function involving both continuity and change, tradition and innovation, and distinct from but related to the broader history of human societies. (If, for example, you've always thought of art as spontaneous self-expression, this view of it may be new to you.)

The job of these units is also to furnish you with enough raw material, examples of art, to enable you to 'do art history' yourself – in other words, to think about certain products of human creativity not only with interest and pleasure, but systematically, seeking out particular types of information, the quest for which itself has a history and tradition which is, as already stated, open to query and innovation.

It's no wonder that no introduction can ever be definitive. (And in a sense even a lifetime's work on a subject can only ever be an introduction.) Although there are wrong ways of embarking on a course of study, ways that stop one from asking fruitful questions or that impose false certainties, there cannot be said to be a single right way. Probably the most important thing to be done in these pages is to alert you to the fact that it has been necessary to make choices on your behalf. These choices are outlined below and an attempt will be made to justify them. You will also be given glimpses of other possibilities. Your set book presents a complementary approach, one that is compelling and important. Although E.H. Gombrich's *Art and Illusion* is a difficult book, it has been chosen precisely because it maps out the history of art in a unique way, posing questions which are basic to the practice and viewing of art and yet which are relegated by some art historians to other disciplines, notably philosophy and psychology. But art history is not a static discipline and views on art and on visual experience have changed since the 1950s and '60s when many of Gombrich's writings were published. There is, for example, a much greater emphasis now on the relationship between art and social and political values, or issues of gender or language.

Although you will be looking at reproductions of works of art and you will be asked to 'think art-historically' about them – which includes doing a fair amount of visual analysis – this introduction will not attempt a chronological survey of Western art from cave painting to the Victorian period in Britain. It will not try to familiarize you with the range of art works which an art historian would expect to know at least superficially. Many of the examples you will look at have been chosen mainly to illustrate arguments. Some of them are considered 'important' by most art historians, others not. Although the course does not assume any knowledge of the visual arts on your part, you might find it helpful, if you have not been doing this already, to start looking attentively at original works of art, in a gallery, in a stately home, perhaps in a historic church or public building in your region. (Remember that the specialist architect, concerned with structural engineering, etc., is a comparative newcomer, and that architecture has been considered a branch of art production throughout most of Western history.) You might also recall our suggestion in the *Course Guide* that it could be helpful to supplement your reading with a good and well-illustrated survey; we recommend E.H. Gombrich's *The Story of Art.* The main purpose of this advice is not to have you learn a great many examples of art, but to help you orientate yourself in what may be an unfamiliar world of images, dates and artists' names. These units and the set text, however, should be given first priority in your reading.

Sections 1–1.6 of Unit 10 are the most abstract part of this *Introduction*. Please do not be tempted to skip them, however, even if you do not immediately see the relevance of some of the questions treated here, and are impatient to get on to working with illustrations. These sections shake up preconceptions which often get in the way of looking at, and learning about, the visual arts. You may even be one of those who has been put off enjoying art by some of these preconceptions as they are enshrined in museums and many publications on art, and you may find that the approach offered here helps you overcome problems which are general but which may have seemed particular to yourself. For these first sections seek to define the subject-matter of art history, ultimately asking the sixty-four-thousand dollar question, *what is art?* This, as you will see, is by no means a closed issue, and the answer we choose to give must affect the way we look at things as well as the way we study the subject.

From defining art the discussion moves on to the various ways of analysing and classifying the visual arts. The focus in Unit 11 is on classification according to genre. *Genre,* a French word adopted in English, meaning 'kind', 'sort', 'type', is an important concept in all the arts, affecting as it does production as much as reception – that is, making as well as appreciating or using. Different criteria apply to the design of, say, a canal lock and a sheep-dipping trough, and we judge these artefacts accordingly; the same is true in the arts, although here the definition of what constitutes a genre (for example portraiture or landscape) is not as clear-cut as in the technological example, and neither are the criteria of success or failure. But even the way traditional generic classifications themselves come into being and are modified is exceedingly telling and an important part of the history of art.

Generic analysis is emphasized for two main reasons. First, the academic study of art should be as concerned with the circumstances of its production as with assessing its impact upon viewers. A study of genre provides valuable insights into these circumstances. Secondly, shared ideas about genre – for example, what expectations we bring to a portrait or a landscape – are one of the most important ways in which meaning is produced and transmitted in the arts.

The search for meaning is a theme which runs through the units. The theme is central because it is assumed that most people, when looking at works of art, want to make sense of them. *What does this work of art mean?* is a question which is cast in many forms: *What does it signify? What is it about? How can we interpret it? What is it saying? What statement is it making?* Such questions are extremely challenging, not least because there is not one single, correct answer. A painting made in Italy in the sixteenth century may have meant something quite different to a viewer at that time from what it means to a viewer in the twentieth century. The way in which we interpret any painting will depend on our own knowledge, experience, expectations, values, society and culture, and on the physical context in which we view it. The meaning of a particular work is therefore *open* and we may conclude that we can describe several possible meanings for it, and some of these may be incompatible with each other.

The search for meaning in a work of art engages the viewer (the beholder) in an intellectual process. This is not to deny that paintings have an effect on our senses or emotions. We may be 'thrilled' by a Rembrandt, 'stunned' by a Van Gogh or imagine the taste of cherries represented in a still life. But these initial responses are only a *part* of what a painting means to us. The search for meaning incorporates and goes beyond these initial clues. It examines the impact of a work on our *mind* and asks: what *facts*, *information* and *ideas* does the work provide? The answer to such questions could be as simple as, 'it tells us what St Paul's Cathedral looks like' or as broad as, 'it demonstrates the fragility of human life', or 'it is a comment on the nature of art itself'. Later in these units (for example, in section 2 of Unit 10) you will find examples of these different kinds of meanings.

Works of art are complex and we should not expect their meaning(s) to leap out at us at first viewing. Meanings have to be built up or constructed from a number of clues. In these units we have tried to indicate the kinds of clues which will be useful to you as you try to place any initial reactions to a work of art (love, hate, wonder, sadness, eroticism, tingling taste buds or plain bewilderment) into a broader framework of interpretation. As you will see, there are many clues to meaning: the way in which artists handle shape and colour; the conventions or traditions, both thematic and stylistic, within which they are working or against which they are rebelling; the social and cultural context and the function of a work both at the time of its making and at the time of its exposure to a given public. In this way, given adequate information, you should also be able to offer reasons for any discrepancy between your own interpretation of a painting and those of other people in other times and places. The crucial point, in all of this, is that we should offer *reasons* for any interpretation(s) at which we arrive.

A final word about the set text, *Art and Illusion*. In theory, visual art need not be synonymous with the representation of the world about us. Architecture, whatever its origins (many people have traced it to the imitation of living forms, of trees for example), is an art which does not seek to imitate other forms of reality. In practice, however, much art in the West and in most of the civilizations of the world has sought to represent external reality, notably to represent in two-dimensions three-dimensional objects in three-dimensional space. The ways this has been done, and the broader implications of changing types of pictorial representation, are the subjects discussed by Gombrich in *Art and Illusion*. Unit 12 will guide your reading of selected passages and chapters from *Art and Illusion*. Professor Gombrich himself talks about some of the central issues in *Art and Illusion* in Radio programme 6.

Because of the emphasis on pictorial art, the architectural plan-reading cassette has not been integrated into the units. You may wish to use this in conjunction with the discussion of personal style in architecture, p.46 in the units, Plate 8 in the *Illustration booklet*. It also has a particular relevance to the section on Urban Architecture in Units 28–29.

Reading art history, whether *Art and Illusion*, or this introduction to the subject, or any other text, is particularly time consuming and demanding, because there are two kinds of 'reading' involved, and both are equally important. There is the customary reading of words, sentences, paragraphs, but there is also the less usual, in our culture, 'reading' of images. Do not be tempted to skimp on this, and be sure to do all the visual exercises asked of you. Only in this way can you develop your own capacity for enjoying art, which, after all, is one of the reasons for studying it.

PACING YOUR WORK ON THESE UNITS

You will find that it is not possible to separate these units into three neat packages, each representing one week's work. Unit 10 is likely to take less than a week; Unit 12 likely to demand more.

When you reach Unit 12 you will see that selected parts of the Introduction and of Chapters 1–5 (inclusive) of your set book, Ernst Gombrich's *Art and*

Illusion are required reading. The rest of the book is optional, but it is hoped that you will be tempted to explore at least *some* of those optional chapters.

AUTHORSHIP

The *Introduction to Art History* was originally written by Erika Langmuir. It has subsequently been revised with the incorporation of additional material, first by Briony Fer and for this version by Linda Walsh.

ACKNOWLEDGEMENTS

Linda Walsh wishes to record grateful thanks to members of the A102 Course Team and tuition and counselling staff who contributed suggestions for and commented upon the revisions to these units. Special thanks are due to Dr Duncan Macmillan, and the editor, Clive Baldwin, many of whose substantial comments have been incorporated into the units.

SET READING

As you work through these units you will need to refer to

E.H. Gombrich (1977) *Art and Illusion,* Phaidon (Set Book)

Illustration booklet (Please remind yourself of section 4.10, 'The reproductions and their captions', in the *Course Guide* before you start work on the illustrations.)

BROADCASTING

Television programme 10 *The Albert Memorial*

Television programme 11 *Cragside*

Television programme 12 *Constable: 'The Leaping Horse'*

Radio programme 5 *Professor Sir Ernst Gombrich on Art History*

Radio programme 6 *Professor Sir Ernst Gombrich on 'Art and Illusion'*

CASSETTE

Although there is no extended discussion of architecture in Units 10–12, it is part of art history and an important element of your studies in A102. There are references to architecture in the units and you are given specific exercises and an introduction to architectural history in Cassette 2, side 2, band 2, *Plan Reading,* and in Television programme 11 *Cragside,* and their associated notes. These are regarded as an essential part of your introductory study of art history. Although there is no specific instruction to work through the cassette at a particular point in the unit material, you should make sure that you do so during the first part of your study of these units and in any case before watching Television programme 11.

Unit 10

DEFINING AND ANALYSING ART

1 TOWARDS DEFINING ART AND THE SUBJECT-MATTER OF ART HISTORY

Art history is an academic discipline conducted, like other arts disciplines, almost entirely through reading, writing and speaking – *verbal discourse*. Art historians conduct their business in verbal language, whether they are trying to describe what happens when they (or others) look at paintings; or they are discussing theories about art, or trying to establish an interpretation of a work; or writing biographies of artists, art collectors or patrons; or discussing the ways in which works of art originate, are produced and used; or debating the politics of art sponsorship. (There are many other issues.) You may feel that some of these topics lend themselves more easily to verbal discourse than others. Most people would feel, for example, that the politics of art sponsorship are best explored through reading, writing and speaking. But what about the experiences we have while looking at a painting? Perhaps works of art present themselves to us purely visually, and if so, it is not easy to see how this visual experience can be translated into words. This introduction to art history, however, is founded on the belief that words *can* help us to describe and analyse our experiences of looking at art as well as to consider broader issues of their history and interpretation.

You may even wish to consider whether 'seeing' and 'looking' are as simple and natural as they sound: can we really isolate the operations of our sense of sight in this way and consider them quite separately from the workings of our mind? In *Art and Illusion* Gombrich points out that all perception occurs in a context of preconceptions and expectations, which we derive from prior knowledge and experience. Gombrich is writing about visual perception in general – the way we orientate ourselves through seeing – but his arguments can be applied specifically to looking at art, particularly if we accept that looking is not passive but involves an effort towards interpretation. When trying to make sense of what we see in a painting, various clues trigger the knowledge and experience stored in our minds. Gombrich's view of art, is, of course, only one among many. Nevertheless, his theories provide an interesting starting point for deliberations on visual experience, and you will be studying them in some detail in your work for Unit 12.

1.1 DEFINING ART

If 'visual experience' is a slippery concept, so is another concept at the centre of our investigations over the coming weeks – *art*. When asked to define *art*, many of us quickly side-step the issue by advising students to consider paintings or other objects in a gallery or museum, or monuments in churches and stately homes. There is, however, a problem with this super-practical approach.

The problem with it is that it conceals as much as it reveals. In the first instance, the contents of museums and galleries are dependent on resources and buying policies. What now appears in any museum is the result of a series of decisions, including what is appropriate and what can be afforded. But there are also fundamental theoretical problems. The most obvious is that it seems inappropriate to ascribe precise contents and boundaries to the conceptual category, *art*. 'Conceptual category' means an idea, an abstract notion, like the ideas of patriotism or love, which can be differentiated from the notions or categories based on generalizing from concrete facts, such as *animal*, *vegetable*, *mineral*. (You probably know the coy attempts at defining *love*: 'Love is never having to say you're sorry'; and, when you think about it, the arguments about what is, or isn't, in the 'national interest' can be seen as trying to define the contents of the notion *patriotism.*) Thus the precise qualities that make an object a work of *art*, like the precise qualities of the patriot or the lover, have been variously defined in different societies and from period to period, and even from person to person or from social group to social group within a single society at any given time. (A notorious case in point was the arrangement of bricks (Carl Andre's *Equivalent VIII*, 1966), bought, at some considerable expense, by the Tate Gallery in 1972. The trustees and directors of the Tate obviously thought of it as an example of *art*; many members of the general public saw it merely as a 'pile of bricks'. The disagreement reveals the difficulty of formulating an incontestable definition of *art*.)

Perhaps less obvious to us is the possibility that some societies have never had *art* as a conceptual category at all. It is most unlikely, for example, that cavemen did. We do not know whether they used their paintings of animals and huntsmen as aids in religious rituals, or as tributes to powerful totems, or as historical records – many such suggestions have been advanced. But, because the paintings are often in normally inaccessible and invisible locations within the caves; because they are neither drawn on specially prepared surfaces nor bounded by borders; because they often overlap and have no common horizontal and vertical orientation; for all these reasons, and in analogy with the products of other tribal peoples, we think that cave paintings were unlikely to have been considered as objects of attention in their own right as distinct from having a function in other social activities and institutions. We should remember, that the conceptual categories and language of cavemen may have been different from our own. Setting aside this difficulty, however, should the probability that cavemen did not produce their paintings with the notion of making *art* preclude us from studying their artefacts within a history of art?

It is now generally accepted that an artefact *may* be classed as *art*, regardless of whether its maker intended that it should be so or indeed whether its maker ever possessed the very concept, *art*. By the sixteenth century we read of connoisseurs collecting, and exhibiting in the reception rooms of their town houses and country villas, paintings originally intended for private devotion and not made to be works of *art*. Such pictures were now hung cheek by jowl with profane works and admired for their appearance and its effects. Indeed, such collections had existed in Graeco-Roman antiquity, and reading about them in ancient texts certainly influenced Renaissance usage. In the Renaissance, as in antiquity, works on devotional themes also began to be produced, with the intention of being viewed primarily as art objects. Look at Colour Plate 1 in your *Illustration booklet*, which reproduces a painting of Mary Magdalen by the Venetian artist Titian (*c.*1480–1576). If you notice an admixture of the erotic in this picture of the penitent sinner-saint do not discount it. This was partly because Titian viewed this devotional subject principally as an art object, but also because in Christian accounts Mary Magdalen was a prostitute who, in an act of penitence, washed and anointed Christ's feet. One of Titian's famed artistic achievements was his painting of sensuous nudes, who combined a thrilling life-likeness with conventions of beauty derived from ancient statuary.

It would be possible to point to many works which could be included under the rubric *art*, despite the fact that, unlike Titian's painting, they were not consciously created as such. Look at Plate 1 in your *Illustration booklet*, which reproduces a ritual mask from New Guinea. The intended function of this object was to frighten women and children in the course of a ceremony in which the young men of the village dressed up as ghosts. The concept of *art* as we know it did not enter into its manufacture. Yet the mainly symmetrical geometric pattern, with its uncanny and powerful evocation of staring and voicing – a striking representation of ghostliness – seems to argue for a conscious desire to create a balanced and effective visual whole on the part of the maker. And we know that there is, or was, a tradition of making such masks in New Guinea, and that a specialist class of skilled craftsmen competed with each other to produce the 'best', the most effective masks. We may be uncertain about the maker's intentions in this case, but the skilful and effective handling of visual form qualifies the object as *art*. In divorcing an artefact from its original purpose, we simultaneously test our perceptions of the object and the perimeters of our concept of *art*.

It is these ambiguities which made Professor Gombrich write in the introductory chapter of his survey, *The Story of Art*:

> There really is no such thing as Art. There are only artists. Once these were men who took coloured earth and roughed out the forms of a bison on the wall of a cave; today they buy their paints, and design posters for the Underground; they did many things in between. There is no harm in calling all these activities art as long as we keep in mind that such a word may mean very different things in different times and places, and as long as we realize that Art with a capital A has no existence. (Gombrich, *The Story of Art*, p. 4)

Gombrich is saying here that *art* is not a universal, unchanging conceptual category. There is no essence or quality which characterizes *art* at all times and in all places: there is no such thing as Art with a capital A. Although his opening statement, 'there are only artists', has been misunderstood by some people to mean that art historians should be chiefly concerned with artists' biographies, he is, in fact, defining art with a small 'a' as a set of *activities* or *processes* (such as 'building' or 'making') in which a certain group of practitioners engage. For this reason, Gombrich continues, the history of art can be defined as 'the history of building, of picture-making and of statue-making'. His definition does not depend on the intended functions of the products of these activities. They might have been meant to be 'works of art' or to help sell shaving soap; we can still study them as products of an artistic process. Equally, according to Gombrich's definition, we do not have to have 'visual experience' of every single product of artistic activity in order to do art history, nor even of particular individual examples. We require 'visual experience' of only enough examples of the products of building, picture-making and statue-making to be able to draw appropriate general conclusions. In view of the losses and destruction of artefacts sustained over the centuries, this is an important consideration.

You may have noticed that Gombrich's definition of *art*, at least as I've quoted it so far, seems to avoid answering the question, *which artefacts are art*? But while denying the existence of an unchanging mental category, *art* (or, as he puts it, 'Art with a capital A'), Gombrich by implication identifies the products of the activities of artists as buildings, pictures and statues – not, for example, calligraphy or gardens, a distinction which will be pursued below (see p.12). In other words, while dissociating himself from the search for an essence distinguishing *art* from other wares of human manufacture – a traditional preoccupation of a branch of Western philosophy – Gombrich nonetheless seems to accept a traditional Western definition of art products. By declaring, however, that *art* is a social construct, that is, an idea which is culturally transmitted, a mental category whose contents vary from social group to social group ('such a word may mean very different things in different times and places'), Gombrich succeeds in adding two important modifications to his original definition of art, as *activities* or *processes*. In so doing he helps us towards a definition of art history: first, he provides the notion that art history is also concerned with chronicling the *changing social functions of works of art* (pictures in caves, advertising posters on the Underground) and, secondly, the notion that art history provides a record of the *changing social roles played by artists* (as designers of advertising posters, helpers in religious rites, or whatever).

However, Gombrich's view of art history is not exhausted by implicitly defining the discipline as a chronicle of *activities* or *processes*, of the changing *functions of works of art* and of the changing *roles of artists* in society. By stating that 'there is no such thing as Art' Gombrich dissociates himself, as already discussed, from the search for an essence – some abstract idea which all products of artistic activity must reflect, however imperfectly, or some quality which they must all share. At the same time, however, he clearly does imply that there is something essentially distinctive about *artists* or about the activities in which they engage, some permanent, common characteristic underlying their changing social roles. If he did not imply this, he could not say 'there are only artists', because he would not be placing all the builders, picture- and statue-makers within the single category, *artists*. And indeed at another point in the introduction to *The Story of Art* Gombrich suggests what this distinguishing factor might be: 'the artist's type of problem'. He thus adds a further item to be included in his – and our – definition of the subject-matter of art history.

1.2 THE 'ARTIST'S TYPE OF PROBLEM': CREATING FORM

There is hardly any person, writes Gombrich in the Introduction to *The Story of Art*, who has not at least got an inkling of the 'artist's type of problem'. Any flower arranger, anyone who has tried to mix and match clothes and accessories, even the cook who seeks the 'right' proportion of custard and pudding on a plate, has experienced 'this strange sensation of balancing forms and colours' to get them 'right' – without being able to tell in advance precisely what 'right' is going to be. Gombrich here touches upon crucially important, complex and contentious issues. 'The artist's kind of problem' he describes is the striving to create a kind of *formal order* through adjusting the relationship between the various constituents which go into the making or assembling of some finished product.

Be sure you note the use of the word *formal* here. This is one of the important words in the art-historical vocabulary. The word is not here used in the sense of 'the opposite of informal', i.e. in order to imply something stiff or tightly structured, but as a derivation from *form* as distinguished from *content*, or *function*. Form can be defined as 'the individual shapes and volumes, and their relationships as depicted in a work of art ...' (Lucie-Smith, *Dictionary of Art Terms*, p.84). However, in practice, discussion of the formal elements of art embraces discussion of colour, line, texture, light, shape and space. The 'artist's type of problem', then, is the arrangement and balancing of these elements. Neither the word, *formal*, nor the concept, is limited to art-historical usage however. Formal literary analysis, for example, will focus on the syllabic and rhyming scheme of poems and on the way in which words are chosen and *arranged*.

Gombrich's description in *The Story of Art* of the basis of artistic activity as 'this strange sensation of balancing forms and colours' to get them 'right' is, of course, contentious. It is loaded with assumptions: firstly, that artistic activity is strange (i.e. it is apart from normal experience); secondly, that it is to do with sensation (rather than with thought or ideas); thirdly, that it is concerned with balance (i.e. with order rather than with disorder); fourthly, that it is concerned principally with forms and colours (i.e. that the balance to which it aspires depends on the organization of particular kinds of abstract or formal qualities); finally, that there is an expectation of rightness which it can satisfy – that it can be judged according to a fixed set of principles shared by artist and spectator. You would find much in more recent art-historical writing to modify these assumptions and these units will, at times, extend or qualify Gombrich's view. Gombrich himself extends and qualifies his views on artistic activity in his later book *Art and Illusion*. Gombrich's ideas in *The Story of Art*, nevertheless, offer a stimulating starting point.

Take, for example, Gombrich's reference to the 'right proportions' of custard and pudding. He is not discussing here how these will taste, or the nutritional value of the dish nor even the ingredients used for making up custard and pudding. He means the way in which the shapes, textures and colours of the two components will appear on the plate. But just as no cook is likely to consider only the visual appearance of food, so no artist (or writer or musician) is likely to think only of the formal properties of his or her work. The distinction between formal considerations and other factors is always only relative, never absolute. There is a relationship between the forms and colours used by an artist and the thoughts and ideas (and therefore possible meanings) implicit in his or her work. Nevertheless, we might agree that Gombrich's view in *The Story of Art* is a useful starting point and that formal considerations figure with especial prominence in the work of artists, that they constitute a specifically 'artist's kind of problem', and that they are therefore central to any art-historical enquiry. The striving for pleasing or effective formal arrangements or for controlled visual effects has been the most consistent criterion of *art* in all cultures which have elaborated the concept. This is not to say that this has been the only important criterion of *art*. As suggested earlier (p.5), the formulation and communication of *ideas* or of *visual information* (for example, about the *relationships* between objects, shapes and colours; about aspects of the world we live in) have loomed large in some areas of artistic endeavour and predominated over the need to create a satisfying *sensation,* or visual effect. Gombrich is more concerned with these other, central aspects of artistic activity in his later book, *Art and Illusion*.

Gombrich believes that the impulse to create formal arrangements is universal – nearly everyone experiences the 'strange sensation of balancing forms and colours' – and that artists, whose professional activity harnesses and exploits this impulse, have existed throughout human history. If this is the case, then art history must concern itself with as broad a range of artefacts as possible and go beyond the study of building, picture-making and sculpture making, to include objects such as the mask we discussed above. It must concern itself also with a host of products of other kinds of processes in which formal intentions play a governing part, from the making of pottery, to weaving, jewel-making, gardening, etc. *The Story of Art*, despite its self-imposed brief, in fact discusses, and illustrates, Persian silk carpets, a Mycenaean dagger, African and Amerindian ritual masks, a Maori house lintel, and other objects not easily classifiable as buildings, pictures or statues.

The circumstances and way of life of any social group limit and direct the artistic opportunities open to it. We cannot, for example, expect nomadic pastoral peoples to erect vast stone monuments, because their way of life involves continual seasonal migration with the flocks on whom they depend for food and most of their raw materials, and because the grasslands through which they range cannot be quarried for stone. And even resettled nomads will continue producing artefacts characteristic of their earlier way of life. We must therefore be constantly alert to our own cultural assumptions about which artefacts are classified as art, or as the products of artistic activity.

Equally, we must be aware of cultural assumptions concerning what constitutes a 'satisfying' formal arrangement, if we accept this as one of the main characteristics of *art*. Such an awareness is perhaps even more crucial in other, less common definitions of the essence or 'main characteristic' of art.

Imagine, for example, the contents of a history of world art which defines art as, primarily, 'that which visibly expresses emotional states', or 'that which instils in us the desire to do good'. Both of these have, as a matter of fact, been advanced as essences, or integral qualities, of all art products. Since the expression of emotional states and ideas of morality are two areas especially dependent on social conditioning, it follows that such definitions of art might preclude us from taking seriously, accepting as worthy of study in the history of art, the products of most other cultures with different conventions and different moral codes from our own. Even if, for instance, ethical ideas were codified in the Maori house lintel illustrated by Gombrich, our own conditioning might prevent us from readily perceiving this. It becomes very easy, with such preconceptions, to dismiss even the most sophisticated and skilled products of other cultural groups as examples of 'craft' rather than works of art. The view of *art* as the product of activities striving for or achieving satisfying formal arrangements is less exclusive in this respect, but not entirely so.

We can now therefore regard the New Guinean mask discussed above as *art*. A hundred years ago or more it would not have been regarded as such, but as an anthropological curiosity. Largely through the agency of modern Western artists' experiments with abstracting the forms of the human face and body, most of us are now able to accept the mask as one kind of *work of art*. We can give it a place on our walls or in our art collections, judging it on its formal merits rather than on its efficacy in village ceremonies of which we may know nothing – just as visitors to the Uffizi Gallery in Florence admire Duccio's, Cimabue's and Giotto's altarpieces without worrying about their original role in Christian ritual.

However, although knowledge of the original function and context of a work of art is not essential to its classification as *art*, such knowledge is necessary for our understanding of its meaning. We have already seen that Gombrich felt the changing social functions of works of art to be a central concern of art history. The social context and function associated with a work of art at the time of its making help to explain why it looks the way it does and to unravel its meanings throughout its history.

1.3 AUTONOMY

To raise the distinction between the function of a work of art and its formal characteristics is to introduce the issue of artistic *autonomy*. Let us first try to clarify the notion of autonomy. 'Autonomous' means 'self-governing', 'self-regulating', 'independent', 'unaffected by extraneous factors and influences'. A helpful analogy is to the self-governance of games. You have assuredly had the experience of playing different games, each with its own rules, and all of them rather separate from the demands of 'ordinary' life outside the game. You will know that the 'rules of the game' specify particular uses within the game of everyday objects – such as parts of the body, or string, matches, etc. – and/or prescribe specialized equipment with which the game is to be played – bats and balls, playing cards, counters and boards, etc. The rules also spell out a conventional set of possibilities and limitations – the string of cat's cradle, for example, or how to score, what is out of bounds or constitutes cheating, etc. Finally, the rules of the game set out pre-determined standards for success and failure – what constitutes achievement, how and when the game is won or lost.

Artists balance forms and colours, strive to get proportions 'right', much as other people play chess or cricket. They too manipulate raw materials – clay, wood, metal, etc. – and use specialized equipment – brushes, hammer and chisel, etc. – with particular ends in mind. Art might be seen as a specialized, self-governing 'game' of arranging colours and shapes. The 'rules of the game' of art are, however, less static, more complex, than those of most games. They are made up of the potentials and limitations of the artist's medium – the wiry line of a hard pencil on paper, of the brittle mass of marble – of the demands of the chosen genre and format – whether it is a life-size full-length portrait, or a marble bust – and of more general aims shared by a group of artists at any given time – such as the need to approximate as nearly as possible the appearance of living creatures, for example. (We shall be considering these topics at greater length below.) The important thing to grasp, at this stage, is that artists are motivated in part by considerations *internal* to *art*, much as the players of games are motivated *in part* by considerations internal to the game. Insofar as artists act according to the internal rules of art, we can say that art practice is autonomous. Artists measure themselves against other practitioners, those of the past as well as those alive today, assessing their own achievements in relation to the 'state of the art' – just like sports-people attempting to break records. They innovate in respect of conventional problems and techniques – just as a tennis player, say, might experiment with a new kind of tennis racket. And only recently have the standards for success and failure, which remain definable in games, become highly debatable in Western art, and 'players' – the artists – and 'spectators' – the general public – have failed to agree on such standards as, for example, the need to approximate life-like appearances in statuary.

We know, from good historical and literary evidence, that even the earliest of artists had a high opinion of their job and were concerned with what we might call formal values in addition to the technical and functional aspects of their works. They competed with each other: look in turn at *The Madonna Rucellai* (attributed to Duccio), Cimabue, *Madonna and Child Enthroned,* and Giotto, *Madonna and Child Enthroned* (illustrations 4, 32 and 33 in *Art and Illusion*); who could doubt that a degree of artistic rivalry – concern with the autonomous aspects of art – played a part in the shaping of these images created for Florentine churches? Given the exact same task, responding to the same external demands of function, scale and subject-matter, working with the same materials and even within the same conventions, such as the larger scale of the Madonna in comparison with the other figures, the three painters nonetheless interpreted their job quite differently. Not only is the way they simulate three-dimensional forms on their two-dimensional picture spaces different; the difference extends to purely formal decisions. Notice the way that Duccio stresses the snaky line of the gold hem of the Virgin's cloak, as it turns and twists from her head down to the pointed toe of her slipper (illustration 4). There is no comparable effect in either Giotto's or Cimabue's altarpiece. Or note the way that Giotto's off-centre placing of the Virgin's halo (illustration 33), more exaggerated than Duccio's subtler effect, creates lively asymmetrical shapes in relation to the curve of the throne's canopy, without breaking up the essential symmetry of the composition as a whole. Cimabue's centring of the halo, on the other hand, serves to emphasize at one and the same time the symmetry of the whole and the gentle inclination of the Virgin's head (illustration 32). These and similar details can be viewed as individual solutions to 'the artist's type of problem', within the (relatively) autonomous realm of art.

The word *relatively* is crucial here. Although some sports people like to insist on the absolute autonomy of games, and some art lovers on the absolute autonomy of art, most people readily perceive that their autonomy *is* only relative. Art *is* affected by factors external to its own specialized world and activities. The nature, status and popularity of games can change, even within single cultures, in response to events outside the game, and many external factors, from the weather to politics, religion and economics, impinge on the playing and watching of games. The external influence of television coverage has made snooker both more popular and more respectable. One-day cricket matches were the result of pressures from sponsors, TV companies, and, perhaps, the patterns of spectators' leisure time. The same limitations of autonomy pertain to art and the appreciation of art. The 'balancing of forms and colours' which lies at the heart of artistic activity cannot be viewed in isolation. Art cannot be described as an autonomous, competitive game. Artistic activity is embodied within a choice and treatment of subject-matter which will resonate and suggest meanings in the minds of both artists and the viewing public in accordance with the human, cultural and economic interests of that artist and public. The Madonna and Child images discussed earlier may have been attempts at a specialized game of balancing shape and colour, but that game was activated and infused by a specific social or cultural need, function, or meaning. We must make a clear distinction between the specialized *means* employed in art (the careful balancing of shapes and colours) and the ends which it serves. (The latter might include, for example, the ambition to comment on social values – an ambition also shared by music, philosophy, and so on.)

There is a long and accomplished tradition in Japan of *netsuke* – miniature wood or ivory carvings, frequently representing animals. But what gave rise to this tradition in the first place was not a formal impulse to miniaturization, but a functional requirement. Since kimonos had no pockets, some secure means had to be found of carrying the small wooden medicine boxes which were a common accessory to Japanese dress. They came to be worn dangling from the belt, tethered by a toggle – the *netsuke*. There are now, however, specialist carvers making *netsuke* for collectors only – not only in Japan, but in the West, where they have never served as toggles. *Netsuke* carving, originally a response to social needs, and carrying a specific social significance, has become an apparently autonomous art activity (although still relying on finding a market for its products, and it could be argued that the market is, in turn, influenced by broader considerations of class and status). Artistic production is sometimes the result of skilled practitioners deploying their specialist expertise, without *apparent* reference to specific social functions and needs; at other times it is firmly rooted in a social function and in a set of meanings which extend beyond the narrow confines of the artist's tools and trade.

You will find many examples throughout the course both of the self-regulating autonomy of art and of the way wider considerations affect the production of works of art, the way works of art look, and even the viewers' responses. Units 22–26, *Culture: Production, Consumption and Status*, look at the ways in which considerations of class and economic status influence artistic production; other units will look at the relationship between Victorian art and the religious, social and moral values of the Victorians. Television programme 12 *Constable: 'The Leaping Horse'*, examines the way in which Constable's depiction of his native countryside was influenced not only by historical traditions of landscape painting which had originated in Italian and Flemish art (factors 'internal to art'), but also how it was affected by contemporary urban (or metropolitan) ideas about rural life (factors 'external to art'). Television programme 18 *The Victorian High Church* shows the way in which religious controversy and ideas of how society should be ordered (both seemingly quite external to art) directly affected the styles of architecture and the decoration of churches in the Victorian era.

1.4 TESTING THE BOUNDARIES OF ART

It would seem, then, that the view of art as a 'striving for controlled visual effects' or as a 'striving for a pleasing or effective arrangement of colours and shapes' is only part of the story. There is a further important issue. If art historians were to limit themselves mainly to chronicling the products of various attempts to balance forms and colours, they would not only ignore the variety of purposes served by art in the past, but would also risk leaving out of their accounts certain recent developments in our own culture (by which we mean, roughly, the culture of industrialized countries).

In our highly specialized environment, some people have been trained (in art schools or other institutions) and practise professionally (through a network of art dealers, art galleries, art exhibitions) as *artists*, but have deliberately turned their backs on the traditional 'artist's type of problem'. They have elected instead to investigate – as it were from within – the whole concept of *art*, and test the boundaries of it as a conceptual category (*art* as opposed to *non-art*). In other words, the products of their activity as artists embody a kind of philosophical enquiry rather than the desire to experiment with formal arrangements. The work of these artists is a comment on art itself and on its relatively autonomous, self-serving qualities. What better way to demonstrate these qualities than by commenting on the ways in which art, in the modern world, has its special, autonomous characteristics reinforced by the context in which it is presented to the public – the gallery. Plates 2, 3 and 4 in your *Illustration booklet* are examples of works which question and comment upon the status of art as a self-serving activity, turning in upon itself and setting itself apart rather than connecting with things external to itself.

A famous historical example is illustrated in Plate 4, which shows a ready-made industrial urinal. Entitled *Fontaine* (*Fountain*), dated and signed with the pseudonym R. Mutt, it was submitted to the first (open) exhibition in 1917 of the Society of Independent Artists in New York by the French artist Marcel Duchamp. At the time it was refused, thus challenging the principle of 'openness'. *Fontaine* was a critique of art as a self-serving exercise in formal arrangements, although it has subsequently become ranked as a classic of modern art. Duchamp tried to kill the notion of the artist as god and the status of the Romantic notion of the artist 'genius'. The 'formal arrangement' of the work is deliberately arbitrary: the urinal was originally intended to be displayed upside-down and subsequent copies were displayed, for example, above doorways. The object was to be neither functional, nor consciously aesthetic, but was intended to raise questions about art and the making of art. As an object destined for exhibition in a gallery, *Fontaine*'s claim to be *art* arises from its proposed context and from its cultural significance rather than from any qualities of shape, colour or texture the urinal itself might possess. Duchamp commonly used ready-mades to de-mystify art and to assert the role of the modern artist as rebel or critic of the established rules of the art game. (This role or purpose had already been adopted, of course, by much earlier artists. Consider, for example, Hogarth's onslaught on the hold of classical conventions and themes on the art world; see *Art and Illusion*, pp. 295–6.) Within this role, artists can question the kinds of prior knowledge and expectation (social, political, aesthetic) which influence artistic production and which Gombrich discusses in *Art and Illusion*. By different formal *means* their art can serve the *purpose* of challenging traditional views and expectations, rather than reinforcing or developing them.

Exercise

What is the significance of Keith Arnatt's assertion lettered on the wall of an art gallery for purposes of an art exhibition and subsequently recorded in photographs (Plate 2 of your *Illustration booklet*) ? Would such a graffito have the same effect painted on the wall of, say, a public lavatory? (When you are looking at reproductions always remember to look carefully at their captions which contain important information.)

Discussion

The context is all-important to the significance of *Keith Arnatt Is an Artist*. At the Tate Gallery, we are unlikely to have read obscene or jokey meanings into this assertion. Our thoughts might turn to the present state of *art* in our society, to the way art galleries, especially state-subsidized ones, art colleges and the whole network of commercial interests in the buying, selling and exhibiting of art, have institutionalized the idea of art for art's sake. Perhaps the inscription suggests: *art* is no longer needed to interpret or represent the natural or man-made world (this function having been usurped by photography, films and television). In addition, the *end*, *purpose* or intention of creating a faithful imitation or effective illusion of the world we see around us seems inappropriate as our own knowledge and understanding of the world grow more complex and uncertain. As the *ends* of art change, so must its *means* or methods. Art has been ousted, or resigned from, its former role as an aid to devotion or to weld community spirit; it is no longer asked to express spiritual or emotional truths, or even to delight; it has become a self-enclosed, self-serving system. Keith Arnatt is an artist because he is a member of the 'art world', having been trained, and being invited to participate in art exhibitions at art galleries.

John Baldessari's inscription, executed for him by a sign writer, stretches across a framed canvas (Plate 3). Unlike *Keith Arnatt Is an Artist*, it assumes the format and employs the materials associated with that traditional Western art product, the easel painting. The most telling difference between this work and another, more 'traditional' painting, Constable's *Wivenhoe Park* (*Art and Illusion,* colour illustration 1), however, is that Constable viewed the easel painting (as did the originators of this form of picture-making) as a simulated window-on-the-world. Constable's painting represents a landscape as it might be seen through a transparent pane of glass, the effects of light translated into a 'code' of paint and brushstrokes. It is meant to evoke in the viewer not only admiration at the artist's skill but also all the associations appropriate to viewing the scene represented. Baldessari's easel painting does not simulate anything other than itself, a stretched canvas supporting painted letters. It even avoids calling into question the artist's technical skill: the letters have been executed for him by a professional lettering specialist. The inscription perhaps directs our attention to the cultural status of the product, easel painting. This portable object, devoid of ideas, of representational skills and even of formal intentions, can be bought, sold, hung on the wall and shown, hidden away; yet it is *art*. Context, once again, is all important: the easel painting is *art* in its historical context and by virtue of its being first exhibited in the context of an art gallery.

In our society, Baldessari and Arnatt seem to be saying, *art* has become impoverished (or, perhaps, the impoverishment is to be understood as being that of society). Stripped of its former power and magic, unwilling or unable to inspire or delight, *art* is reduced to self-perpetuating institutions and marketable commodities and, perhaps, jokes for the in-crowd. It does not much matter whether or not these interpretations are the 'right' ones. The meaning of things is never simply reducible to the meaning intended by the maker. Perhaps we should resist the temptation to read too much pessimism or opportunism into these works. Nevertheless, as these products have been made by trained professional *artists* within the context of *art institutions*, they need to be considered within the history of art, even in their deliberate rejection of formal intentions and effects and in their deliberate refusal to please. (However, even the limited choice of typography, placement, scale and colour or tone demonstrates how difficult it is altogether to abolish formal considerations in planned visual effects. It is probably to further distance the 'artist' from these considerations that Baldessari left the lettering to a 'craftsman'.) Thus we see that even a broadly cross-cultural definition of art as the product of activities largely governed by formal intentions and effects is inadequate, since it cannot encompass 'artistic' activities resulting in such products as those reproduced in Plates 2, 3 and 4. These works are *art* because of their context and because of the ideas they generate within that context: they demonstrate the way in which context and cultural significance can supersede formal considerations in our distinctions between *art* and *non-art*.

It seems that professional art historians must include in their definition of the subject-matter of their discipline such responses by professional artists to the question, *what is art*? This is not a question of taste but of scholarly integrity. Insofar as art history chronicles these responses, it abandons its ostensible role of investigating the properties of a finite set of artefacts (works of art) and itself becomes a constantly evolving philosophical enquiry. In this way art historians join many contemporary artists in their paradoxical activities: using the apparatus of art institutions in order to question the role of art in our culture, to clarify the social and political implications of the modern museum, of the market, of the systems which support them.

1.5 BEAUTY AND QUALITY

It may have occurred to you that the words *beauty* and *quality* have not yet entered into our discussions of *art*. Art can be beautiful, ugly or anywhere in between these two extremes. Hogarth's satirical representations of eighteenth-century life are judged to be works of art, despite their preoccupation with physical and moral evil (*Illustration book*, Plates 58–9). The search for 'beauty' is one – but only one – of the ideas long associated with *art* in the Western tradition. Notions of what constitutes beauty, however, are singularly vulnerable to changes in fashion, even more so than notions of morality. (We are not, of course, debarred from finding beauty in many different kinds of objects, and probably, however we define beauty, the sense of profound pleasure to which our experience of it gives rise is universal.) Changes in concepts of beauty, are certainly subjects of art-historical enquiry. Static prescriptions for universal beauty (for example, in order to be beautiful a painting must have qualities x, y and z) on the other hand, are not.

Quality in art, although sometimes used as if it were synonymous with beauty, is something quite different. The problem of defining quality is unresolved: it is likely that we will judge a work to be of high quality when it meets our needs, which may demand qualities as diverse as entertainment, emotion, flattery, knowledge, nostalgia, a display of skill, pleasing colour, social status, and so on. Arguably, quality has to do with the degree of complexity and richness achieved by the artist: the breadth of references on which he or she is able to draw, the seriousness of the problems posed by his or her activity in relation to our perception of the human condition, the difficulties, both technical and conceptual, overcome, the balance struck between traditional and innovative solutions. Solutions to formal problems can, for example, be skilful and effective, without giving rise to the 'sense of profound pleasure' associated with beauty.

However, the quality of artistic production is not the responsibility of the artist alone. It is their society and culture which provide artists not only with a tradition, but also with opportunities to perform their dazzling feats. And if society offers only trivial opportunities, reduces the artist's activity to barren and superfluous gestures, then that society makes the production of art of high quality impossible. Some would argue that it is despair at what they perceive to be their inability any longer to engage in art of lasting relevance which underlies many contemporary artists' acts of social protest. Perhaps, however, such views discount the positive and creative nature of much artistic 'rebellion' (such as Duchamp's *Fontaine*).

The category *art* thus admits the possibility of 'bad art' alongside art of high quality, and does not restrict the concept of *art* only to products of high quality. Some art historians feel that discriminations of quality are somehow incompatible with disinterested scholarship, while others are willing to make value judgements. Just as political historians are not compelled to admire all the developments they chronicle, so art historians, it seems, should be able to acknowledge a preference for some forms of art – whether or not made with the intention of being *art* – above others. In fact, the scholarly study of art history is one of the best ways to learn to appreciate quality in art. Knowledge of artistic processes, of the varying functions of art products, of the various roles played by artists, of the choices they face, can furnish us with a guide to artistic achievement in a way that 'simple' visual experience, overlaid as it is with unexamined assumptions and historically incongruous expectations, cannot.

1.6 SUMMARY: WHAT IS ART?

Are we now in a position to hazard a definition of *art*? If you are still hoping for a hard and fast rule you will be disappointed. The question, *what is art?* is not the same sort of question as *what is water?* Water is a substance of very particular properties, and which exists even before we enquire into it; an exhaustive answer will always include its molecular composition, the fact that it is liquid within a certain range of temperatures and pressures, its natural occurrence in rain, etc. Our question, *what is art?* is not, however, of the same kind. *Art*, unlike water, is not a substance with a set of distinctive factual properties, and its existence does not precede our ability to ask about it. It is true that cave paintings and altarpieces exist, like water, independently of our naming of them. But the category *art* does not. Water is a substance with a real existence. *Art* is a mental category devised for intellectual purposes. As Gombrich writes, 'There is no such thing as Art'. *Art* isn't a *thing*, it's an intellectual category. Western culture, and very few other cultures, such as those of the Far East, have had a conception of *art* when drawing up a mental map of the world and human activities. Other cultures have not.

Let us grant, however, that the concept always includes objects either made, or modified in some way from their natural state, by people. Sunsets, however beautiful and emotionally moving, are not *art*, although we may choose to analyse our experience of them in terms analogous to our experience of works of art. There are thus, it seems, two possible ways of answering the question, which products are *art* products?

1 Those artefacts or modifications to the natural state made or planned with the intention of being *art* (with consciousness of the category *art* as opposed to *non-art*, and/or in the context of art institutions – this allows us to include Arnatt's graffito, alongside examples of more 'traditional' art);

2 Those objects, etc. which, while not made in the knowledge of the concept *art*, or not intended to be included within the mental category *art*, are subsequently classified as such (for example, the New Guinean mask discussed above).

In practice, such a categorization has usually meant attending primarily to the formal qualities discernible in a work, or to its cultural significance. Note that this definition of art excludes notions of quality or beauty – such judgements being seen as subjective or culturally conditioned rather than universal.

In reaching such definitions the *viewer's perception* takes precedence over the *maker's intentions*. Intentions never exhaust the potential significance, or meaning, of an artefact. Viewers' perceptions are conditioned by their expectations, and these expectations, in turn, are affected by the *context* in which artefacts are viewed. *In practice*, artefacts looked at in an *art* context (such as an exhibition in an art gallery) are scanned for qualities such as formal pattern and viewers tend to attribute artistic intentions to the makers, ignoring other intentions. When the intention to create a pleasing or effective formal arrangement is explicitly denied (as is the case with both Plates 2 and 3) viewers are urged to re-examine their assumptions about art. Thus they are forced to admit that, *in theory* (and in the limited practice of certain artists) the intention to create a pleasing or effective formal arrangement is not an essential ingredient of *art*.

In later sections there will be more about the rise of art institutions (which have been rather taken for granted here) and their influence on the theory and practice of art in the West. The second part of the course, in which you will be studying Victorian Britain, investigates the network of art institutions in this country in the nineteenth century, and the way Victorians grappled with their notions of *art* and *non-art*.

Having established the broad basis for a definition of art, it would be appropriate to conclude this section by defining what, as a consequence, is seen to constitute the subject-matter of art history. Art history is a history of:

1 Artistic processes – that is, of how works of art are produced. (What materials, techniques and conventions are available to the artist?)

2 The varying functions and meanings of art products, both at the time they were made and later – for example, the Underground poster which starts life as a commercial advertisement and ends up in a museum. (Viewers' perceptions and expectations and the role of institutions are crucial here.)

3 The special but varying roles played by artists in society – which may include biographies of individual artists, but also more general investigations of the social functions and status of artists, as well as of what they are asked to make. (Art is only *relatively* autonomous.)

4 The different ways in which artists have approached and resolved formal problems, within and beyond the restraints of convention. ('Competition' within the 'rules of the game'.)

5 The ways in which art has been defined over the ages.

2 THE ELEMENTS OF PAINTING

In sections 1 and 2 of Unit 8 you learned to identify the elements of music and to assess their importance and effect within specific pieces. It is important to develop similar skills in art history (where there is sometimes a *loose* connection with the terminology of music), concentrating this time on looking rather than on listening, and on learning to describe what you see. Previous sections have emphasized that the autonomy of art is only relative: a complete examination of any painting must take into account the function, context and meaning(s) associated with it both at the time of its production and in subsequent periods. Before you can undertake this kind of broad analysis, however, you will need to develop some expertise in discussing those elements of art central to the artist's special 'game' or 'trade': that of organizing and balancing colours and shapes. By becoming more proficient in this area, you will gain more confidence in *interpreting* paintings, for it is the particular way in which visual elements are handled in a painting which help us to understand what it 'says' or means. It is important that you work through the exercises below and devote some time to looking carefully at the reproductions discussed in order to gain an understanding of the way in which different artists approach and resolve formal problems and choices and in order to learn what we might describe as the 'language' of painting. Restrictions of space mean that we can only concentrate on painting (rather than, say, sculpture or architecture) at this point, but Cassette 2, side 2, band 2, *Plan Reading,* should help to familiarize you with the language of architecture.

2.1 PICTORIAL ANALYSIS: IDENTIFYING AND DISCUSSING THE ELEMENTS OF PAINTING

(a) Colour

SOME WORKING DEFINITIONS

As you work through these definitions, you will need to refer to the colour wheel reproduced in Figure 1 (following page 24). When looking at the colours used by an artist there are a number of factors to take into account.

Hue is the term used for the spectrum name of a colour. It is that attribute in respect of which we speak of colour as red, blue, yellow, etc. The word *hue* can be used in reference to the three primary colours (blue, red and yellow) and in reference to secondary colours, and other mixtures. *Secondary* colours are produced by mixing equal proportions of two primary colours. Thus, blue and yellow produce green; blue and red, violet; yellow and red, orange. Other mixtures or *hues* include green-blue, yellow-green, orange-yellow, red-orange, red-violet, blue-violet. A **complementary colour** is a primary colour which, when placed beside the secondary colour produced by the other two primaries on the colour wheel, appears brighter or stronger. (For example, red is complementary to green; blue to orange; yellow to violet; see the colour wheel, Figure 1.)

Intensity or saturation refers to the degree of brilliance or purity of a colour: we are more impressed by the 'redness' of a colour which is pure red than by that of a red which has been mixed with grey. A pure, vivid colour is said to have a high *chromatic* value (from the Greek *chroma* meaning colour).

Local colour is the colour inherent in a particular object.

Modulated colour is colour that has been modified by light, shadow or reflections of colour from adjacent objects.

Tone refers to the degree of lightness or darkness in a colour. (For a broader usage of *tone,* see below, p.24.) Some colours are inherently brighter (i.e. have a brighter tonal value) than others: yellow is brighter, less dark than violet. A colour can be tinted in order to make it darker or lighter (i.e. in order to change its tonal value). For example, the addition of white will brighten a colour – but this will also affect the chromatic purity or saturation of the colour. The grey segments on the colour wheel chart the degree of light or dark in each of the colours represented, irrespective of hue. The word *tone* is also used loosely, and occasionally, in reference to the prevailing hue in a picture.

Temperature is used to attribute imagined warmth or coolness to a colour. We often feel that reddish-yellow colours are warm (like fire), blue-greens cool (like ice). These impressions are, however, relative. As with all the other attributes of colours, their warmth or coolness is accentuated or played down in accordance with the other colours which surround them in a painting. The relative temperatures of colours can be used to give convincing effects of depth and volume; light, warm colours tending to advance towards the eye and cool ones to recede. (The colour wheel indicates colours in the range from warm to cool.)

LOOKING AT COLOUR IN PAINTINGS

Exercise

Please look at *Great American Nude No.99* by Tom Wesselmann (Colour Plate 13 in the *Illustration booklet*). Although this is not simple, try to set aside the subject of the painting and make some notes on the nature and effect of colour in this painting.

Discussion

On first looking at this reproduction, you may have been struck by its vividness and its flatness: there is little impression of depth behind the picture plane (the imaginary vertical plane which coincides with the physical surface of the painting, see below, p.27). This effect is generated by the use of colour. Fields of pure ('saturated') colour juxtaposed in this way tend to flatten the overall effect: look, for example, at the red lips. On careful scrutiny, however, we see that the hues of the cushion, in the foreground, the rose in the background and the blue-green 'disc' (cushion?) on the right *are* modified ('modulated') in a somewhat artificial and limited way, by the use of light, shade and (in the case of the rose) other hues. This adds a strange, slightly disturbing three-dimensionality to a primarily two-dimensional painting. Areas of colour which are modulated by light and shadow, or by reflected colour from adjacent objects are generally more suggestive of recession into space. Where areas of colour are modulated in this way and therefore change from one tint to another across small distances, the term 'atmospheric colouring' is often used. The large patches of pure colour in this painting are the opposite of atmospheric colour.

An artist can achieve a more powerful, dramatic effect by choosing and juxtaposing colours from opposite sides of the colour wheel (complementaries): the contrasting colours seem to vibrate and compete for our attention. (You will find further discussion of this painting on pages 106–7 below.)

Exercise

Please look at the following reproductions:

Nicolas Poussin, *Landscape with the Body of Phocion Carried out of Athens* (Colour Plate 12)

William Dyce, *Pegwell Bay* (Colour Plate 27)

James McNeill Whistler, *Nocturne in Blue and Gold* (Colour Plate 59)

How does the use of colour in these paintings compare with that in the Wesselmann?

Discussion

In each case the range of colours used is (a) narrower (b) more harmonious (in the colloquial sense of 'well fitted together' and not in the technical musical sense), and (c) less bright or vivid. We must be very careful of course, when reaching such conclusions on the basis of printed reproductions. It is very difficult to record the chromatic value or precise hue of a colour in a painting through the photographic process. The ageing process can also, of course, modify the original colour values of a painting, particularly when varnishes susceptible to yellowing have been applied to it. (Many of the white clouds depicted in J.M.W. Turner's paintings are turning yellow-going-on-brown; for an example of a painting by Turner, see *Art and Illusion*, illustration 240.) Nevertheless, it is clear that our three artists have here selected colours, within each painting, which are close to one another in the spectrum or colour wheel. This generates a feeling of harmony or visual 'peace' against which the smallest notes of discord or difference stand out vividly. 'Peace' and 'harmony' may therefore be some aspect of the meaning to be derived from the visual elements of these paintings. The title of the Whistler painting derives from Chopin's *Nocturnes* ('Night scenes'): like the music, the painting evokes a hazy, dream-like night scene. The neutral colours of the Dyce make the red of the woman's cloak and the distant sunset stand out more than they would have done in a painting of more vivid hues: the same might be said of the splashes of gold in the Whistler. Note how the small patches of red stand out against the more neutral browns and greens of the Poussin. Compare these with *The Leaping Horse* (Colour Plate 16) by Constable, who established a reputation for adding small, but striking patches of red against complementary greens.

The colouring of all three paintings is subtly modulated or 'atmospheric' in that it changes from one hue to another across small distances. This has the effect of making us peer more closely into the detail of the paintings (as opposed to the striking 'poster effect' of the Wesselmann, which we are inclined to view from a distance). There is a greater sense of 'reality' in the colours of these three paintings: they conform more with our experience of the world as we view it. (How many pure colours can you see around you at the moment, and how many others which are the results of a mixing process or which are modulated by light, shade and reflections of the colours of adjacent objects in some way?) In the Whistler the subtly modulated colour of the water adds an impression of depth. (Is there less three-dimensionality in the more uniform colour of the bridge?) In the Poussin the warm (advancing), subtly modulated greens and browns suddenly give way to the cool, (receding) blues of the distant hills and sky. (Does this sudden transition of hue and tone add to the dream-like quality of the scene, another clue to its meaning?) The harmony, tranquillity and serenity of the colouring is partly due to old coatings of varnish and the pervasive yellow-green film it produces. The painting appears monochromatic (in a single colour) in places (the same green, modified slightly by additions of black or white). The subtly changing colours invite meditation and contemplation in a way in which more vivid contrasts might not.

(b) Tonality (light and shade)

(N.B. There is little direct connection between tonality in art and tonality in music. In the latter, *tonality* is a term relating to musical keys.)

SOME WORKING DEFINITIONS

Tone and **tonal values**: terms used to indicate the lightness or darkness of a colour, picture or area of a picture. We can assess the tone of a colour or picture independently of its hue(s) (see above, pp.21–2). Black-and-white reproductions help us to see which areas of a painting are dark, light, or mid-toned, without any reference to the hues of the original.

Chiaroscuro (Italian for 'light-dark'): the balance of light and shade in a picture; the skill shown by the painter in the management of shadows. The word tends to be used mainly in connection with painters like Rembrandt and Caravaggio whose works are predominantly dark in tone (see Rembrandt, *The Young Haaring, Art and Illusion,* illustration 29). In these works light seems to shine onto areas of the canvas rather than emanating from or through the objects it depicts.

Tonal range and **gradation:** the tonal range of a painting is the distance (in terms of brightness) between its lightest and darkest sections. This range might be narrow in a subtly harmonized painting, broader and more contrasting in a more dramatic painting. *Tonal gradations* refer to the transitions between light and dark areas. When used in a subtle way, such gradations of tone in surfaces turned away from the light can suggest three-dimensional form and volume: light and shade can 'model' (i.e. suggest the three dimensions of) form. Subtle tonal effects are normally incompatible with intense, brilliant colour.

LOOKING AT TONE IN PAINTINGS

Exercise

Look at the following reproductions:

Ford Madox Brown, *The Pretty Baa Lambs* (Colour Plate 34)

Caravaggio, *The First Saint Matthew* (Plate 24)

William Dyce, *Pegwell Bay* (Colour Plate 27)

Compare the tonal values of these paintings.

Discussion

'Bright and sunny' are my first impressions of Madox Brown's *The Pretty Baa Lambs.* The figures and animals seem to absorb the frontal glare of the sun. (This brightness is one of the effects of the Pre-Raphaelite technique of painting onto a white ground (first layer of paint).) There are none of the strong contrasts of light and dark introduced into painting by Leonardo in the fifteenth and early sixteenth centuries and imitated by succeeding generations of artists; but then, such contrasts and 'old master gloom' were regarded by practitioners of the Pre-Raphaelite style as a sign of artistic decadence. Although some areas of *Pretty Baa Lambs* are *relatively* dark when compared with others, no area is dark or gloomy in an absolute sense. The

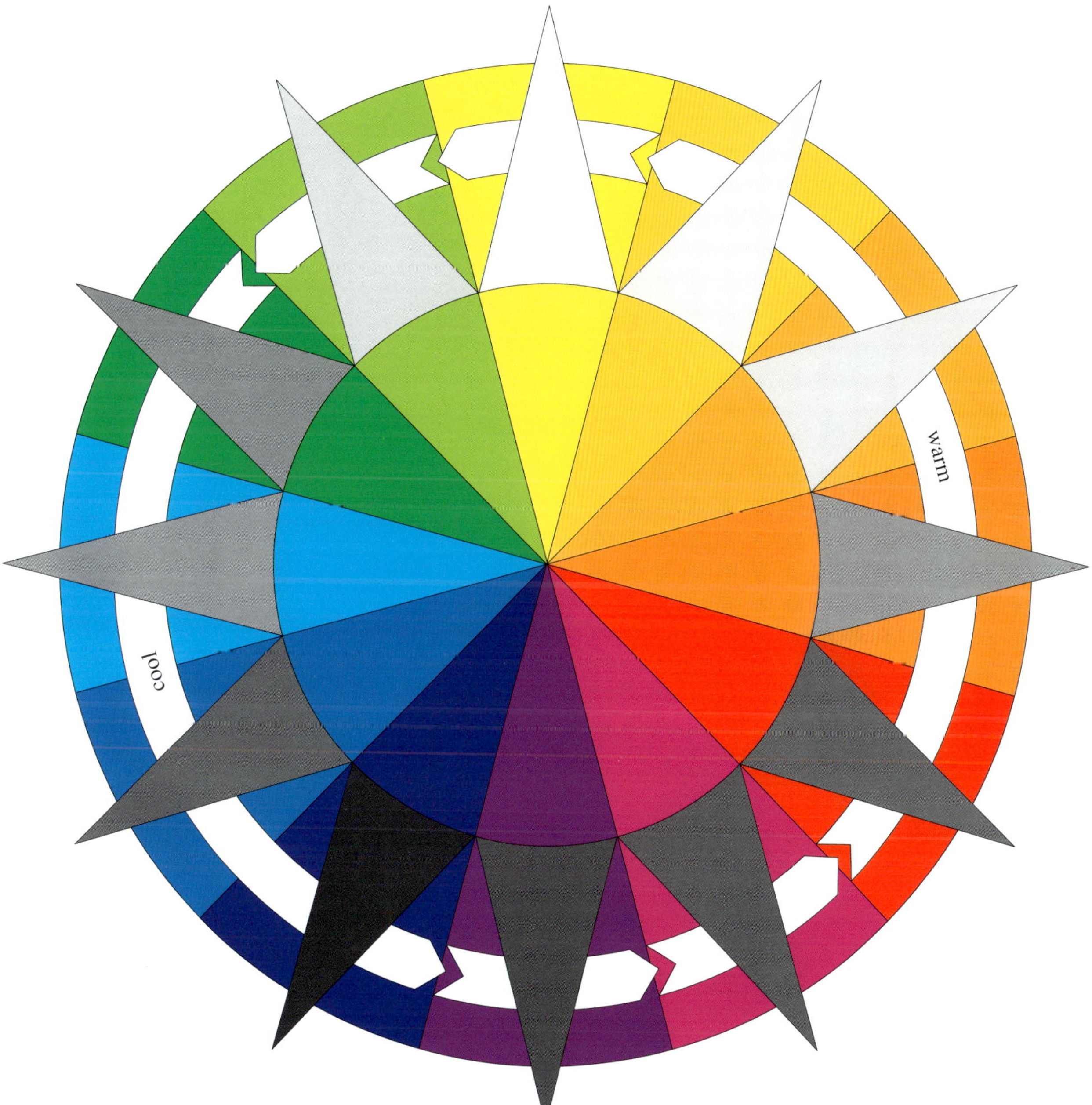

Figure 1 Colour wheel. (Taken from Piper, D. (1984) *The Joy of Art*, Mitchell Beazley, p.108. © Mitchell Beazley Publishers, 1984, 1981.)

mid-tones of the landscape serve to enhance the radiance of the central figures. Shadows are cast, but the open vista and cloudless sky keep these to a minimum. This work was painted outdoors in order to capture the real qualities of the full light of day. As you will hear later in Television programme 22 *The Leathart Collection*, Madox Brown rejected all suggestions of religious or 'celestial' meanings in the work. He caught sunstroke while painting it and the job took so long that the sheep ate the flowers.

In the Caravaggio, by contrast, parts of the central characters seem lit by a strong, raking light so that they emerge, in dramatic relief, from the gloom. The tonal range in this painting is much broader, the chiaroscuro exaggerated, leading to striking contrasts between the brightest and darkest areas. The contrasts are softened, however, by gentler tonal gradations in parts of the painting: in the drapes of Saint Matthew and the angel, for example. In paintings like this the traditional association of light with the divine, holy and beneficent and of dark with death, evil and spiritual anguish, seems to add extra force. Our attempts to find meaning in such paintings depend on our familiarity with the relevant conventions.

In *Pegwell Bay* light is used, perhaps, in a more poetic (evocative) and subtle way than in either of the two other paintings. A pallid autumn light suffuses the composition, softening the contrasts between rocks and sea in the middle distance. There are extremely subtle tonal gradations in the sky, water, cliffs and beach: the gentle sunset glow enhances the beauty and wonder of the spectacle and makes us more receptive to broader meanings concerning time and nature, about which you will learn more in later units.

(c) Line and texture

SOME WORKING DEFINITIONS

Texture: (i) the quality of the paint surface in a picture (connected with the way in which an artist has mixed and applied paint); (ii) the imagined quality of the surfaces of the objects depicted in a painting (e.g. rough, smooth, shiny, dull, thick, thin, metallic, flesh, wooden, etc.); (iii) the rhythm of the brushstrokes (loose, tight). The texture of a painting can link visual and tactile impressions: we can imagine what the surface of the objects depicted, or of the painting itself, feel like. (Note how there is *some* overlap here with *texture* as discussed in relation to music: musical textures can be light or heavy, thick or thin. There are, however, more specialized applications of the term in both art and music.)

Line or contour: the boundary of any two- or three-dimensional shape as seen from any given angle. **Linearity** is the reliance on line for the principal effect in a drawn or painted composition. Most paintings include contour(s) to which our sense of shape can respond, but some contours are sharper or more clearly defined than others. (Look for example at illustrations 24 and 25 in *Art and Illusion*, where the contours of the face in Fantin-Latour's painting are much clearer than those of the Manet painting.)

Masses: 'The simplest, largest and most fundamental shapes to which the component parts of a painting ... can be reduced' (Lucie-Smith, *A Dictionary of Art and Artists,* p.267). Some artists (for example, Velasquez) tend to work with masses or areas rather than with line or with clearly delineated ('drawn' with clear contours or outlines) shapes. This approach, where paint is applied in indeterminate patches of colour rather than contained within clear, sharp lines or outlines, is described as **painterly**. Its opposite is described as a **linear** style (see above).

LOOKING AT LINE AND TEXTURE IN PAINTINGS

Exercise

Look at the following:

John Constable, *The Leaping Horse* (Colour Plate 16)

Ford Madox Brown, *The Last of England* (Colour Plate 24)

Compare the use of line, mass and texture in these paintings. You will have to take into account the fact that texture is often difficult to see in reproductions.

Discussion

The surface texture of the Constable is characterized by thick dabs of paint, loosely applied. There is no attempt to hide individual brushstrokes here. The artist's hand is evident in the thick, broad application of paint and the brushstrokes are varied in accordance with the textural surfaces depicted: broad and loose for the roughness of the wood; delicate dabs for the leaves in the trees. This adds, perhaps, to the appeal to the senses generated by the painting -- to our sense of touch in particular. We could say that texture suggests meaning here, in that it helps to describe the qualities of the natural scene represented. Although the contours of shapes in *The Leaping Horse* are clearer than those of the full-size sketch represented in Colour Plate 15, the finished work is conceived in terms of mass rather than of line: it demonstrates the 'painterly' manner. The picture is divided, broadly, into three masses, or coloured shapes, perceivable even to half-closed eyes: clouds, trees and landscape. Rough, uneven textures slow down our scrutiny of a painting – permitting, perhaps in this case, our imaginative engagement with the scene depicted (TV programme 12 *Constable: 'The Leaping Horse'*, discusses the way in which Constable's loose brushwork was not immediately acceptable to the Academy, which demanded in the works they exhibited a greater degree of 'finish', i.e. a smoother picture surface in which individual brushstrokes were not so evident.)

The Last of England is linear rather than painterly: the edges or contours of figures and objects are more clearly defined or 'hard-edged'. This 'hard-edged' quality was typical of the first phase of Pre-Raphaelite art and constituted a conscious objection to the 'slosh' or loose brushwork of many old masters: a technical equivalent to what was regarded as their moral degeneracy (Brown was not one of the Pre-Raphaelite Brotherhood, but moved in their circles). The textures of flesh, hair, vegetables and textiles are lovingly and carefully depicted in this painting, but with fine, careful brushstrokes, resulting in a more smooth or polished picture surface. Brown's wife had to stand in the yard in winter so that he could observe and render correctly the cold-weather flesh tones. The careful drawing or contours ('sharp focus') of the painting allows us to read it quickly and to imbibe its moral seriousness: but is the unremitting clarity of line (a) oddly unrealistic and (b) distracting? (Note how even the background detail, which might be a little blurred in real life and vision, is as sharply defined as the foreground figures.) Which approach do you find the more effective in the rendering of the textures of cloth, rope, wood, foliage, etc. – Constable's or Brown's? Does your answer depend on the distance from which you view the reproductions? Which approach makes it easier for the beholder to derive meaning from the paint on the canvas?

(d) Scale or size of image

The dimensions of a work and of the figures and objects within it can have a profound effect on the beholder's response. This is discussed further in

Unit 11, p.43. (Always remember to look at the captions for the reproductions in your course material as they give you important information, including the dimensions of the work.)

(e) Composition

SOME WORKING DEFINITIONS

Composition is, broadly, the effective *combination* of elements in a painting to create meaning. It is the broadest of the 'elements' we have looked at so far and incorporates many of them: it embraces the combination and arrangement of colour, light, shape, figures and objects. Typically, an analysis of the composition of a painting would include the ways in which various elements (such as linear perspective (discussed below), scale, tonal range, etc.) 'organize' the picture space by suggesting recession *into* space (depth) and by suggesting relationships between the different sections and planes of a painting, between foreground and background, etc. These factors, as well as arrangements of colour, influence the way in which the viewer's eye is led into or across the canvas. (There are connections between the idea of visual composition and musical *form*, discussed at length in Units 7–9. Indeed, a broader use of the term *form* in relation to art, for example formal order, as discussed above, p.11, can be used interchangeably with composition.)

Picture-plane: 'The imaginary plane represented by the physical surface (canvas, paper, etc.) of a painting' (Lucie-Smith, *Dictionary of Art Terms,* p.146) (The flowers in the bottom left-hand corner of Holman Hunt's *Our English Coasts* (Colour Plate 25) appear to be on the picture plane, whereas there is an illusion that the head of the white sheep in the bottom right-hand corner projects out beyond the picture plane, towards the viewer.)

Picture space: apparent space (or depth) *behind* the picture-plane, created by the use of perspective and other devices.

Perspective: method of representing a three-dimensional object, or a particular volume of space, on a flat or nearly flat surface.

Linear perspective. This quasi-mathematical system, also known as **optical perspective**, was invented in Florence in the early fifteenth century and is based on the fact that parallel lines appear to converge and objects appear to become smaller the farther they are from the viewer. Imagine, for example, the way in which the margins of a straight road (or the parallel lines of a chessboard) appear to converge when we look along its central axis: these parallel lines will eventually recede to meet at a point level with our eyes. The horizontal line on which this convergence occurs is called the **horizon line** and the points at which any receding parallel lines appear to meet on it are called **vanishing points**. **Centralized** or **one-point perspective** occurs when the eye is drawn to a single vanishing point in the centre of a composition. Many early applications of perspective theory were based on a fixed, monocular (one-eyed) artist's viewpoint (it was common for artists to use a peephole device when plotting a perspective grid; see *Art and Illusion*, illustration 244). This represented a simplification of the way in which we view scenes and objects in real life, where our binocular (stereoscopic) vision rapidly scans a scene, and our heads and eyes move frequently. Because of this, many artists have tried to apply perspective theory in a less rigid manner. Linear perspective is not, of course, a major element in all paintings. In many, for example, there is no clearly defined horizon, eye level or viewpoint. (If you would like to go into the finer details of perspective, please see Alison Cole's book listed in the References at the end of these units.) Figures 2–5 illustrate some of these points (see pp.28–9).

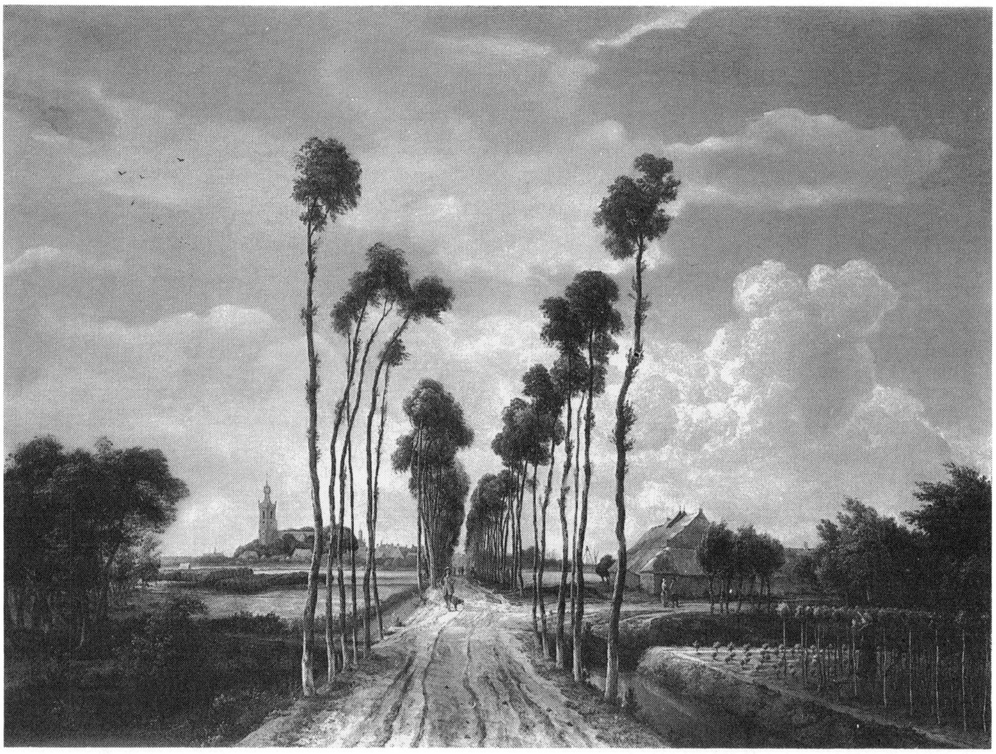

Figure 2 Meyndert Hobbema, The Avenue, Middelharnis, 1689, oil on canvas, 104 x 141 cm (40¾ x 55½ in.). National Gallery, London. This painting is an excellent example of the use of one-vanishing-point perspective. The parallel lines formed by the tops and bases of the trees appear to converge near the head of the man walking towards us: this is the vanishing point. There is a clear horizon line along the base of the village and extending to both edges of the painting. Our eye level is the same as the man's – we might meet him any moment. Note also how objects and people reduce in scale with distance. Reproduced by courtesy of the Trustees of the National Gallery.

Aerial perspective, or **atmospheric perspective**, is the suggestion of distance and recession in a painting, achieved as a result of the way in which the atmosphere affects human sight. With distance, outlines become less precise, small details are lost, hues become more blue, colours become paler and colour contrasts less pronounced. This optical effect is caused by light being absorbed and reflected by the 'atmosphere': a mist of dust and moisture. This mist is most dense at the Earth's surface, where it scatters light and causes distant tones to lose contrast. Blue light penetrates the mist most easily, making the sky appear blue and giving distant objects a blueish cast. The artist can duplicate this effect through the use of light and colour, thereby creating a sense of depth.

Exercise

Comment on the effect of linear perspective in the following paintings:

Ford Madox Brown, *Work* (Colour Plate 29)

Emily Mary Osborne, *Nameless and Friendless* (Colour Plate 30)

Sir Edward Burne-Jones, *King Cophetua and the Beggar Maid* (Colour Plate 58).

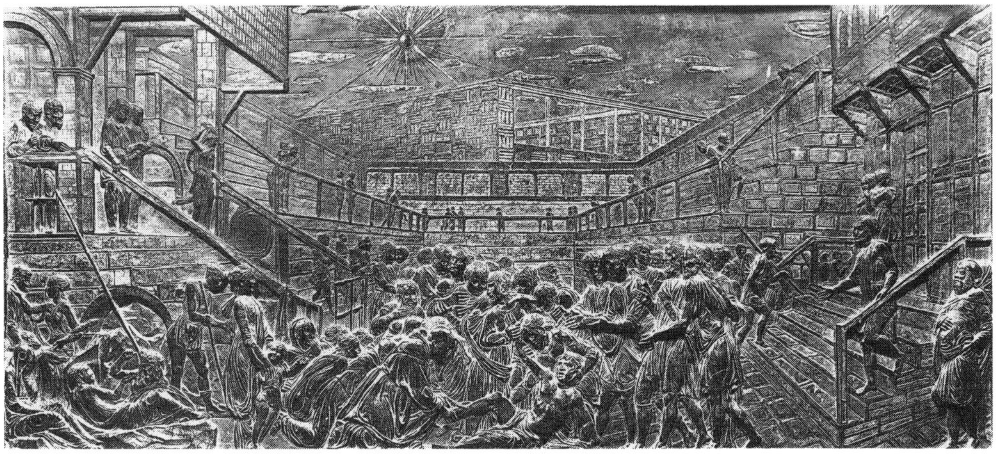

Figure 3 Donatello, St Anthony Healing the Young Man's Foot, 1446–53, bronze panel, with gold and silver, 57 x 123 cm (22½ x 48½ in.), high altar, Basilica S. Antonio, Padua. (See the perspective diagram in Figure 4.) Photo: Alinari.

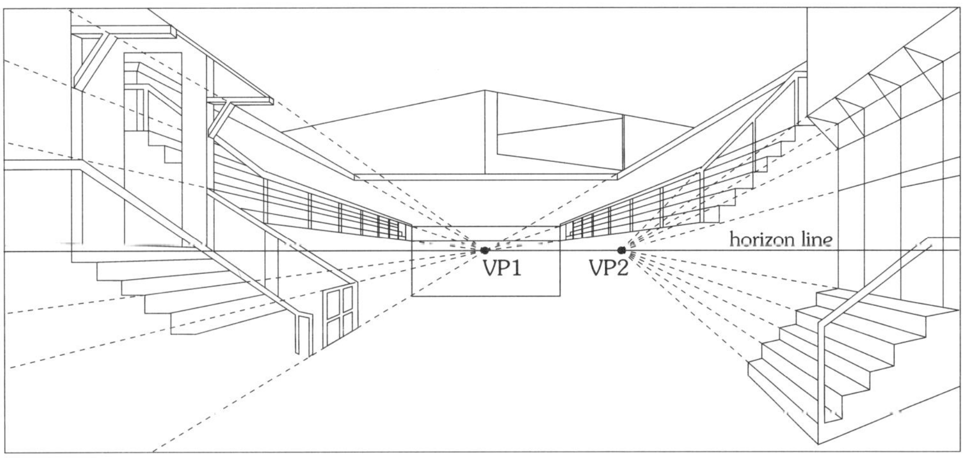

Figure 4 Diagram showing the perspective lines of Donatello's St Anthony Healing the Young Man's Foot. *Where the objects depicted are not parallel with or perpendicular to the picture plane, like the bases of the buildings in Donatello's panel, which are at an angle to the picture plane, more than one vanishing point (VP) is used. Note how both of the vanishing points in this panel meet on the same horizon line. The building on the left-hand side and the stepped stand on the right-hand side meet at a central vanishing point (VP1). The building in the right foreground leads to a vanishing point further to the right (VP2).*

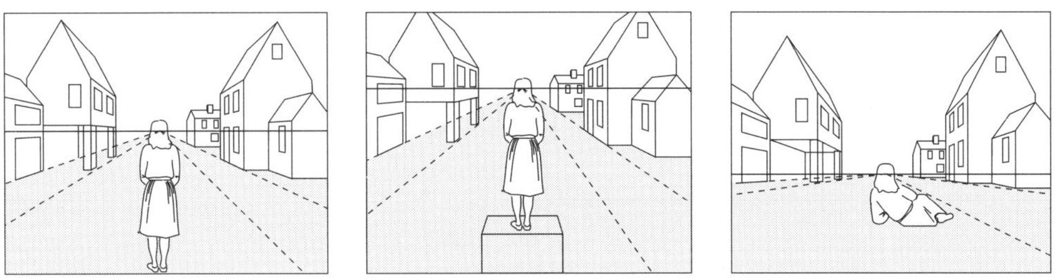

5a Normal viewpoint.
The horizon line of a painting always corresponds with the spectator's eye-level. Here, where the spectator is standing on the horizontal plane known as the ground plane, the horizon line is at head height.

5b High viewpoint.
The spectator is now raised above the ground plane, standing on a box, and looking down at the same scene. The horizon line is at the higher eye-level, and the spectator can now see more of the ground plane.

5c Low viewpoint.
As the spectator is now lower down, the eye-level, and therefore the horizon line, are also lower. Less of the ground plane is now visible.

Figure 5 The effects of different heights of viewing point.

Discussion

In *Work*, as in the other two paintings, linear perspective creates an impression of depth or recession into space. The margins of the road in which the navvies are working, parallel in reality, appear to converge, their point of convergence (and therefore our eye level) being the head of the gentleman on horseback. He is at the apex of the triangle or pyramid, both physically and socially. This could be another instance where the handling of visual elements or techniques suggests meaning – in this case about social status. Figures are reduced in size in accordance with their distance from the picture-plane, intensifying our impressions of depth and distance. In Burne-Jones's painting, the parallel banisters above the beggar maid's head would converge, if extended, at a point just to the left of her right elbow, as would the converging lines of the steps below her. This makes our eye level somewhat lower than the maid's gaze: the perspective encourages us to look up at her. Our gaze is not quite as lowly, however, as that of the King. What does this suggest about the relationship between the two figures? In *Nameless and Friendless* the converging lines of the counter meet at a point behind but level with the child's head (as do the converging lines of the carpet and of the painting hung on the right-hand wall). The horizon line and our eye level are therefore similar to that of the child and we can 'look up' at the superior gaze of the man inspecting the painting in the same way. Again, the use of perspective helps to suggest social relationships between figures.

Exercise

Compare the composition (or general 'layout') of the following paintings:

Nicolas Poussin, *Landscape with the Body of Phocion* (Colour Plate 12)

John Everett Millais, *A Huguenot on St Bartholomew's Day* (Colour Plate 38).

Discussion

The picture space in Poussin's painting is very deep (there is a sense of distance behind the picture plane) whereas that in Millais' work is very shallow – literally 'walled off' – on a plane not far beyond that of the picture plane. Thus in the one painting we have a sense of distance, space and vastness; in the other a claustrophobic space in which the two lovers are forced or 'pushed' close to the picture plane, allowing us to scrutinize the intensity of their poses, of their expressions and of their relationship. Composition suggests broader meanings about the human relationships depicted. The figures in *A Huguenot on St Bartholomew's Day* are bound together into one, imposing, central motif. They occupy a large proportion of the canvas. (The Huguenots were French Protestants. St Bartholomew's Day of 1572 saw the massacre of Huguenots first in Paris and then through France as a result of an attempt by ruling Catholics to exclude Protestant factions from power.)

Composition can refer, as we said earlier, to the arrangement of colour and light, as well as to that of space and shape. The rich textures and vivid sections of the costumes of Millais' figures, as well as their flesh tones, make them stand out from the less vivid hues of the background; the light falling on the girl's face makes her a focal point. In Poussin's painting the only striking colour notes are those of red against green/brown. The figures are much less substantial – almost insignificant in the context of the grand vista and city in the painting, which adds significance to the shroud (also 'spotlit') covering the general's body in the foreground. (Phocian was a virtuous Athenian governor denied a funeral by ungrateful and vindictive compatriots.) There is a careful layering of horizontal planes in the painting, which enhances the impression of vastness and invokes contemplation. Distance is mainly suggested through the reducing scale of figures, trees and buildings. The use of aerial perspective is more limited than that of many paintings by Poussin's contemporary, Claude Lorrain, in whose work there is often a cultivated, *gentle* transition from dark foreground tones to bright background tones. There is, perhaps, something slightly unreal about the relationship between light and shadow in the painting which, in conjunction with the grand vista and tiny figures, is conducive to philosophical reflection on the lot of humanity.

The elements of painting can work together in this way, mutually reinforcing a particular effect or meaning. They can, on the other hand, contradict or counteract one another, in order to create tension. One artist, Jean Fautrier (1898–1964) used 'pretty' pastel shades in depicting the mutilated bodies of Nazi hostages in Paris (for example, *The Jewess,* 1943).

Unit 11

AN HISTORICAL SURVEY OF THE RISE OF GENRES

1 CLASSIFYING ART: THE GENRES

In Unit 10 we concentrated almost exclusively on the visual qualities of paintings: on the ways in which colour, light and shape are arranged within them. We have already hinted, however, that it is not really possible (or healthy!) to discuss formal elements in isolation in this way. You will have noticed, in the pictorial analyses in Unit 10, that there appears to be a causal relationship between formal elements and the meanings generated by a painting. Thus we spoke of the messages about harmony implicit in the use of colour in Whistler's *Nocturne in Blue and Gold*; of the contemplation of the human condition suggested by Poussin's use of colour, light and perspective in *Landscape with the Body of Phocion Carried out of Athens*.

If an assessment of the formal elements of a painting assists us in our search for meaning, this is also true of our attention to the *content* and *subject-matter* of a work. Our recognition of the story of Phocion in the Poussin painting, for example, and a knowledge of that story, assists us considerably in our attempts at interpretation. Furthermore, we often discover that there is a powerful link between content, formal elements and meaning in a work of art. Artists choose and arrange colour, light and objects in a manner appropriate to the subject they are treating and to their own interpretation of that subject. An artist who wishes to produce a lifelike image of a bowl of fruit will handle composition, colour, light and shape very differently from an artist who wishes to produce, for example, a large-scale landscape painting (as in Constable's *Leaping Horse, Illustration booklet*, Colour Plate 16). If we can perceive this relationship between form and content, we are better equipped for our own efforts at interpretation. Those efforts are further assisted when we learn that there have, in the past, been quite strong traditions regarding the *appropriate* formal treatment of certain subjects. By respecting, or rejecting, or transforming, such conventions artists can generate meanings appropriate to their own context.

There is a scheme of classifying works of art which can help us here. As you know from your own experience, in order to study something one must have a framework, a way of dividing up the subject into manageable chunks. Classification is generally based on schemes which, it is hoped, reveal genuine relationships in the items classed together. Botanists, for example, study *plants* ('any of the group of living organisms which typically do not exhibit voluntary motion or possess sensory or nervous organs ... as distinguished from *animals*'), which they tend to classify according to common structure and ancestry.

When thinking about classification it is crucial to remember, however, that schemes of classification occur in a context of preconceptions and expectations on the part of the classifier, rather than being simply inherent in that which is classified. Indeed, it has been argued that our perception of the world *is* a system of classification: we see what we look for, align it with ready-known categories, attend to what we expect or hope to find. Just as our perceptual system is ultimately governed by our need to maintain life, so also our intellectual schemes of classification are founded by our interests. An agriculturist might classify plants by whether or not they will grow in a given climate or a particular soil; a food gatherer classifies plants by whether they are edible or poisonous.

A scheme of classification which can help us in our interpretation of painting is *generic classification* or *classifying art according to genres*. When we classify art according to genres we classify it according to *subject-matter;* we make a decision about what kind of art product we are dealing with. The French word *genre* means 'kind' or 'type'. 'Landscape' and 'still life', for example, which are familiar today, are *types* of subject-matter, or *genres*.

Before we can distinguish between 'different kinds of art product', however, we need to be aware of the *repertoire* (range and kind) of art products characteristic of each period and location. Different *subjects* were popular at different times, partly because of the different purposes or functions served by art. There is a close relationship between the *genre* (type of subject) of a work of art and its function. Only when you read an exhaustive account of, say, art production in the area around Paris in the twelfth century do you learn that it was mainly involved with the building of new episcopal town churches; that the ideals and aspirations of society focused on erecting structures 'half-way between heaven and earth', their function being to embody in stone and glass the Christian community in the heavenly Jerusalem. Still life, on the other hand, a form of painting which became firmly established in the seventeenth century, lent itself readily to the function of decorating secular domestic spaces and became an important vehicle for experimentation with pictorial representation of texture, volume and shape. In a later period, Cubist art exploited and subverted the characteristics of this genre.

Genres tell us about the kinds of choices available to artists and about the society in which they work. A second advantage in studying art through generic categorization is that it draws our attention to the expectations and criteria we apply as viewers: we expect different qualities of a still-life painting than of a narrative (story-telling) painting. Genres are important ways of transmitting traditions in the arts and preserving the (relative) autonomy of art. In her recent work on eighteenth-century portraiture, Marcia Pointon has discussed how artists' attempts to describe character and personality were hampered by 'the prosaic demands of the genre' (*Hanging the Head*, p.47). She was referring to conventions governing format, pose, setting, and so on. Genre dictates, or at the very least affects, formal intentions and the appearance of works of art.

Since the generic repertory of any society – that is, the type and range of the subject-matter of art works produced by that society at any given period – results from the interplay of tradition and current requirements, a survey of the genres of Western art provides a good point of entry to the study of artistic processes, of the varying functions and significance of art products, of the special but varying roles played by artists in Western society and of how meaning is constituted in the visual arts – the subject-matter of art history as defined in Unit 10 (see pp.19–20).

2 FROM CIRCA AD400–CIRCA AD1500: ICONIC AND NARRATIVE IMAGES

The points made in this section are very schematic. Between 'antiquity' and the 'Middle Ages' there is not the abrupt gap here suggested, nor are artistic conditions as uniform as the following scheme would indicate. Nevertheless, this scheme is true in its broad outlines, and provides a useful skeleton which you can flesh out as you gain experience in art history. You can supplement your reading of this section, if you wish, by consulting a good survey, for example, Chapters 8 and 9 in Gombrich's *The Story of Art.* These give a brief but less schematic account of European art between the sixth and twelfth centuries.

By the period known as Late Antiquity – roughly speaking the fourth century AD – European civilization clustered in urban centres around the Mediterranean had attained a stage of art production and utilization not unlike that which we know today. That is, in addition to the public use of sculpture, painting and monumental architecture for political and religious ends, there was a vast consumption among the privileged classes of art for private use. This was partly commissioned, often for commemorative purposes, and partly bought on the open market. The very rich had art-historical collections anticipating our own public museums and galleries; earlier and even exotic art forms were prized, collected and copied. Virtually all the genres of images concerned with representing the visible world that are known to us today – portraits, landscapes, still lifes – had their counterparts in ancient Graeco-Roman art. A major difference is that the important technique of reproducing images through printing was unknown, and the use of visual images for teaching and transmitting information was thus minimal.

This situation altered radically in the Early Middle Ages (from about the late fifth century) with the collapse of urban civilization in Western Europe and the rise of the Catholic Christian Church to a position of secular as well as spiritual power. The Church was ambivalent towards visual images. Monumental statuary, especially when it was free-standing, was associated with idolatry and the rule of pagan emperors. As it ceased to be commissioned, so it ceased being produced, with a consequent loss of expertise. The private art market slowly ceased to function, except to purvey a restricted range of devotional articles or items for personal adornment. The skills of builders and 'makers' came to be directed almost entirely to the task of erecting and embellishing churches and convents, purpose-built for use by the religious and transmitted in debased form though the illustration of the Gospels and other devotional texts in monastic scriptoria, workshops set apart for scribes and copyists (see for example *Art and Illusion*, illustration 50).

An exception to the predominantly religious subject-matter of art was the architectural specialism in military fortifications and the elaboration of armour and weaponry which occupied many artificers. Decorated pottery and plate, heraldic art, tapestries and various embellishments for palaces were other significant areas of artistic production. In addition, a shrinking population, decimated through the wars, plagues and famines attendant upon the collapse of the Roman Empire, and the gradual erosion of the institution of slavery, fostered the search for other sources of power as alternatives to human labour. We might guess that some of the sort of people who would formerly have become artists, that is, professional 'visualizers' and 'makers', now turned to various forms of engineering. It might help you, in your later work in art history, to recall that the distinction between *art* and technology (as well as *art* and craft) is a very recent one, and that before the eighteenth century the design and execution of major projects of architecture, sculpture and even painting were not thought to require very different qualifications from those required to design and execute bridges and roads, systems of irrigation or drainage, offensive or defensive engines of war, etc. (This leads us to further, interesting comments on Gombrich's view in *The Story of Art* that the basis of art is the 'balancing of forms and colours'. As his later book, *Art and Illusion,* shows, drawing has been, for centuries, the basic discipline of art. It is not 'special' to art, however: it is widely used today in engineering, architecture, geography, geology, botany, medicine and a range of other fields of scientific, technological and academic study.)

We can thus say that, roughly speaking, in the Middle Ages, much of the art of Western Europe was dedicated to the service of Christian dogma and liturgy. There was, therefore, one principal *genre* or kind of subject-matter: religious. Attempts to oust from the Church imagery representing the human form, for fear that it echoed pagan idolatry, ultimately failed. But the Church's mistrust of the magical, seductive power of images (which might lead people to worship the image itself rather than direct their devotion *beyond* the image to the Divinity represented), helped to create an art which did not attempt to copy the world of three-dimensional appearances but merely acted as a system of signposts to transcendental and unchanging truths. The skill of faithfully imitating the world of external appearances was replaced by other artistic skills, better suited to the new purpose attributed to art. Church buildings were adorned with figurative decoration, i.e. with schemes of decoration based on depictions, however altered or distorted, of elements of the visible world – for example, the human form, plants, other motifs. These elements were interpreted within the context of sacred history and doctrine, whether in mosaic (Colour Plate 2; *Art and Illusion*, illustration 100), mural painting, or in relief and near-relief sculpture (Plates 5, 6), so that each individual church became a symbol of the one Universal, Catholic Church itself. The Church, in turn, symbolized the New Jerusalem, the Heavenly City of which Saint John the Divine speaks in Revelation, Chapter 21. We can classify these religious images in two types: the *iconic* and the *narrative.* Both types can be found in association with architecture when on the monumental scale, and in manuscripts and liturgical objects when small.

It is possible to regard these two categories as *sub-genres* within the period we are currently discussing, as they deal with significant and specialized categories of subject-matter under the broad heading of 'religious art'. Religious icons take very specific representations of Christ, the Virgin Mary and the saints as their subject-matter; religious narratives represent stories or events from the Bible and sacred history. We could even sub-divide further each of these categories (for example, within 'religious narratives' can be categorized other, significant groupings of art according to subject-matter, such as the annunciation, the crucifixion, the fall of Eve.)

As *genres,* both religious icons and religious narratives continued to be important for some considerable time beyond 1500 AD. Nevertheless, the terms *iconic* and *narrative* have a broader significance and application. These terms are often used, not to denote a distinctive and separate *genre* or category of subject-matter in art, but in reference to the particular 'job' a painting is doing, to the function it is fulfilling (for example, in the case of narrative art, telling a story or in the case of iconic art, graphically expressing the essence of something). Thus any art with a story-telling function or purpose – representations of events from the daily lives of seventeenth-century Flemish peasants, from the heroes of Homer, from a contemporary soap opera – can be described as *narrative*. Similarly, the term *icon* is often applied to an image which stresses the timeless, hieratic (formal and 'sacred') aspect of its subject, allowing maximum eye contact of the viewer with the image. *Iconic* tends to denote static, frontal figures, sometimes with exaggeratedly prominent eyes. More broadly still, an *iconic* image shares some of the essential, characteristic aspects of that which it signifies: Marilyn Monroe is, perhaps, a striking *icon* of twentieth-century stardom and Andy Warhol's portrayals of her may be described as 'iconic'. It has been said that the aim of many modern sculptors is to create an *icon* (i.e. a timeless symbol) of 'the unknown dimensions of feeling and sensation' (Read, *Modern Sculpture,* p.212).

2.1 ICONIC IMAGERY

Let us consider *iconic* imagery first. Please do not, as many people do, confuse the words *iconic* and *iconographic. Iconography* is the systematic investigation of subject-matter, as opposed to style, and is much broader in meaning than the term *icon*. It may mean delving into the symbolism of particular images (for example, the lily – symbol of purity – is part of the iconography of the Virgin Mary), or classifying the types of images used to represent particular persons, scenes or places. Such a search might range across works in a number of *genres*. The iconography of Elizabeth I, for example, might draw upon different *kinds* or *genres* of images – portraits, historical narratives, and so on – in which Elizabeth is present. The content and symbolism of the pictures in which she was present would be the primary interest. Thus the *iconography* of Christ includes images of Jesus as an infant in scenes of the nativity or adoration, as a grown man on the cross or being taken down from the cross, at the entombment, as judge in scenes of the last judgment, etc. It would *include* specific, iconic representations of Christ (highly conventionalized images of Christ, symbolic of his inner essence).

Like iconography and iconographic, *iconic* derives from the Greek work *eikon*, meaning 'image'. An *icon* embodies the essence of the personage by depicting his or her significant, essential qualities and attributes (symbolic objects conventionally used to identify a particular saint or deity or their qualities) and status, but not at any particular moment or in any fleeting state of mind or being. *Iconic*, as used in art history, refers to this kind of depiction.

An icon is therefore a specific, narrow category within the broader iconography of a particular subject or person (for example, Christ). A single personage may be represented in different attitudes (poses), and with different attributes, but these signify, not momentary states (moods, preoccupations, emotions, actions), but different aspects of the essential being (for example, holiness, majesty), and are thus identified by name.

Much Byzantine art of the East Roman Empire (5th century AD to the fall of Constantinople (formerly Byzantium, now Istanbul)) was iconic. Look, for example, at the mosaic reproduced in Colour Plate 2, made by Byzantine craftsmen in the twelfth century to decorate the apse of a church in the Norman Kingdom of Sicily, but based on earlier conventions evolved in Constantinople. The large half-figure in the conch (semi-dome) represents Christ in Majesty. This particular type of iconic image of Christ is called *Pantocrator*, the Greek word for 'Ruler of All'. The frontal pose, staring eyes, the blessing right hand and the Gospels held in the left hand are characteristics of the Pantocrator type, which recurs in thousands of icons. The standing full-length figure of the Virgin below, her arms raised in the Greek gesture of prayer, is also a familiar iconic type: the *Virgin Orans*, or 'Virgin praying'. Neither of these figures is to be understood as performing a transient action at any particular moment of history. Majesty, authority and prayerfulness are *essential aspects* of Christ and of the Virgin *for all eternity*. Thus, while the *iconography* of Christ (described above) may include images which tell the *story* of Christ's life, an *icon* of Christ embodies and declares his essential qualities *outside* the context of any particular story or event. The figures of the angels flanking the Virgin, and the Apostles in superimposed ranks below, are perhaps more easily grasped as simply *being* – not doing, or experiencing, or expressing anything other than their existence. It would be inappropriate to ask, 'where precisely are they standing?' 'what time of day is it?' 'what season of the year?' 'what has just happened?' 'what will they do next?' These are all *iconic* figures. Exactly the same is true of the royal saints represented in sculpture on the jambs of the west portals (doorways) of Chartres Cathedral, *c.*1145–70 (Plate 5). They are shown holding books or scrolls, but we do not feel that they picked up these objects some time ago and will put them down presently. Like their crowns and haloes, these are attributes of status. They say something about the eternal qualities and messages embodied in the saints. *Iconic* imagery (always using the word in its art-history sense only) is concerned with the status of the personages it represents, and some particular aspects or quality of their being, as it were frozen in time or outside time altogether. It may also be used to represent *personifications*, that is, representations in human guise of abstract notions – like the statues of virtues and sciences on the Albert Memorial discussed in Television Programme 10.

2.2 NARRATIVE IMAGERY

The concept of *narrative* art is easier to grasp. The chief aim of a narrative painting is to tell a story. Look at the panel from the bronze doors of Bishop Wernward at Hildesheim Cathedral in Germany, completed in 1015 (Plate 6). Adam and Eve are being reproached by God the Father after eating the fruit of the Tree of Knowledge. If we know the biblical account we can easily interpret their actions: the Lord points an accusing finger at Adam, who covers his nakedness with leaves and cowers, pointing at Eve: 'The woman did tempt me'. Eve, on the other side of the fatal tree, blames the Serpent at her feet. An action over time and in time, that is, an action with a 'before', 'during', 'after', as all stories have, is unfolding before our eyes. The image may only be able to capture one moment, but it is obvious that this moment relates to a sequence of events. This particular story takes place within Christian sacred history, at a particular moment of that history, but not all narrative paintings (particularly those of later periods) are concerned with the famous stories of history: others are concerned with the stories of ordinary people. In all narrative (story-telling) paintings, it is appropriate to ask, however, when and where these events occured, what the people taking part did, what they felt.

Iconic art demands that the spectator recognizes the qualities and status of the subject depicted. In the sphere of medieval religious art, its purpose was to inspire awe and veneration. (A similar purpose might be ascribed to Muslim and Hindu iconic images.) *Narrative* art demands rather more of the viewer. From simple recognition of the story, we may be expected to experience a whole range of emotions: empathy with the protagonists, the desire to learn from what is being depicted – either deploring it and vowing to do better, or wishing to emulate the noble deeds represented.

Typically, then, medieval representation recognized two major categories: the *iconic* image of the Godhead, saints or, in a secular vein, rulers; and *narrative* scenes from the Gospels, the lives of Christ and the Virgin, and the exemplary lives of saints or (less frequently) secular heroes. Sometimes both types figure within a single pictorial field, as in the early altarpiece of Saint Francis shown in Plate 7. The large iconic figure of the saint is flanked by smaller narrative scenes showing key events from his life and miraculous deeds after his death.

The line between iconic and narrative imagery is not always as clearly drawn as in these examples. The image of the crucified Christ may be part of a narrative scene of the crucifixion, or an icon in its own right, as when the crucifix stands on the church altar, representing Christ the Saviour who died for the sins of human kind, and whose body is eaten, whose blood is drunk, in the Eucharistic mass. Sometimes a single image can be read as both iconic and narrative, as, for example, in the many carvings of the last judgment which appear above the west portal of twelfth-century churches. In these, Christ performs a temporal act of judging, and is surrounded by lively narrative scenes of the blessed and damned, angels and devils – yet is represented as an immobile, iconic figure, Christ the Judge. Nevertheless, the distinction is usually obvious and extends, as already said, also to the secular art of the Middle Ages and beyond. (There are, for example, iconic images of monarchs as well as those of saints.)

A compound type of imagery is also important in the medieval period only. These are allegorical (symbolic or emblematic) images, which are part figurative (depicting forms and motifs of the visible world) and part diagrammatic, and which borrow features from both icons and narrative. You may have seen examples, such as the Tree of Jesse motif of stained glass windows, in which the pedigree of Jesus is traced through little 'ancestor' figures perched on a tree sprouting from the midriff of the sleeping Jesse. Or you may be familiar with the Wheel of Fortune: a king enthroned atop the wheel, falling off as it rotates, reappearing as a ragged beggar under the wheel, and rising again on the other side, an emblem of human fate. One moment we are kings, the next, beggars. Illustration 106 in *Art and Illusion* illustrates a model for just such an image. But however dear to medieval artists, these compound representations tended to be replaced by images which were either *iconic* or *narrative*. Note that the term *allegorical* is not as strong or as specific as *iconic*. *Allegorical* may refer to figures, objects or stories used to describe or symbolize other things or events which are suggestively similar. For example, a skull may symbolize mortality; a classical figure may represent Time or Truth; episodes from mythological or literary texts might be illustrated as exemplary of virtue, or of vice and its consequences. Such images, while symbolic, are not as formulaic, sacred, or awe-inspiring as icons.

Specialists in medieval art naturally recognize and study different categories of art products, from cathedrals to castles, from mosaics and frescoes to illuminated manuscripts and embroidered textiles, from stone sculpture to ivory book covers and engraved gems, secular works as well as religious. But for our purposes in these units we need to distinguish only two categories of Early Medieval and Medieval art: the iconic and the narrative.

Iconic and *narrative* describe two very different types or functions of art: the representation of eternal qualities or essences, considered outside the passage of time, and the telling of a story unfolding in time. At this point, you might like to do an exercise which focuses on the way in which iconic and narrative images require a different handling of colour, space and shape, that is, a different approach to the elements of painting.

Exercise

Look at the following:

Artist unknown, *Pantocrator, Angels, the Virgin and the Apostles* (Colour Plate 2)

Artist unknown, *Adam and Eve Reproached by the Lord* (Plate 6)

Compare these, making notes on what you can deduce from them about the artists' intentions. Consider in particular how the artists may have wanted to influence the viewer's response to the image. Be sure to take into account the setting in which the original images were viewed.

Discussion

Let's begin with Colour Plate 2. You should have noted at least some of the following points. The setting is the main apse of a church: Christian dogma provides the context within which distinctive features are depicted. Christ the Ruler of All is represented *above* all the other figures, and *bigger* than they. We might say that he dominates the pictorial field as he dominates Christian dogma. In addition to the details already indicated above (p.37), the blessing right hand, the book in which inscriptions in both Greek and Latin proclaim, 'I am the Light of the World', you might have noted the cross inscribed in his halo. This cruciform nimbus is reserved for representations of Christ. You might also have noted the Greek letters IC and XC on either side – the monogram of the Greek spelling of *J*esus *C*hrist. These letters, and all the other captions in Greek – the monogram of the Praying Virgin, the names of the Archangels and of the Apostles below – like the captions on posters (see p.44) serve not only to identify individual figures but also tend to deny that the gold background on which they are represented bears any resemblance to reality (Real space, real air and light do not have disembodied letters floating through them.) This sort of arrangement has been called 'Christ's Heavenly Court': the Archangels on either side of the Virgin are indeed dressed in Byzantine court robes. It is probable, however, that their dress is, like their wings, an attribute of their heavenly status, and no resemblance to a particular heavenly scene is intended. Specific times and places are not relevant in iconic art. The figures are related to each other conceptually and decoratively on the wall rather than in pictured space.

Christ's frontal pose has already been mentioned (p.37). He and the Virgin are both represented in full-face, and their eyes are accentuated: larger than realistically plausible, outlined with dark rows of tesserae (the little cubes making up the mosaic) and highlighted with lighter lines on the cheekbones and forehead. The effect – certainly one intended by the artist – is that we are drawn to make eye contact with these figures; Christ in particular is staring at the viewer. His size means that he seems to stare straight at us, whatever our position in the church. None of the other figures avoids our gaze, but since they are shown in three-quarter face, none solicits it as urgently as Christ or the Virgin.

It would seem that no overall reading of the mosaic is suggested. The apostles may or may not be read as 'in Heaven'. They simply, and literally, stand 'between' us and Christ. The Virgin is higher than they. The symmetrical arrangement ensures her instant visibility above the window, and gives her pride of place. The disparity in scale between Christ and the other figures does not, perhaps, tempt us to ask what his precise physical relationship is to the others, or even whether he sits or stands. The decorative bands between the registers are seen for what they surely were: a way of dividing up the wall surface to enable all the figures to be placed on it.

Even the precise expression of the most visible figure, Christ, is ambiguous. In a dark church, with the gold and jewel-bright colours of the mosaic shimmering softly in the light of candles from the altar, we are free to project onto him the response we wish. Some writers have singled out for praise his loving and compassionate air, others his austere severity. What matters is the supreme paradox of his distance from us, in scale, through space, in majesty, and the intimacy with which, despite that distance, he seems to look into the innermost soul of each one of us.

Despite being cast in monochrome bronze, the relief reproduced in Plate 6 seems far more realistic than the multi-coloured mosaics of Colour plate 2. We tend to ignore the purely decorative abstraction of the 'vines' to left and right, and read the frame of the relief panel as defining real space in which figures and the Tree of Knowledge (botanically pretty fanciful) are placed. Notice the way in which the right foot of God the Father overlaps the bottom frame: as a result his left foot seems to be set deeper inside three-dimensional space, giving this figure greater appearance of depth than the actual shallowness of the relief, and defining his spatial (and psychological) relationship to Adam and Eve, cowering slightly 'behind' the frame. I've already outlined the actions and reactions of the participants in the narrative (p.38); notice in addition the way the sculptor has clustered the Tree, Adam, Eve and the Serpent, and isolated God the Father. His accusing index finger is the main point of contact between him and the others. One does not, perhaps need much cultural conditioning to read or interpret the poses of Adam and Eve as lacking in self-confidence: crouching, their bent knees signalling instability of posture, hiding. Everything in the pose of God the Father: raised arms, firm legs, thrusting head, speaks at the very least of resolution. What the artist lacked in anatomical competence he more than made up for in vigorous command of body language. If we cannot, perhaps, empathize at a very complex spiritual level with this representation, we can surely do so at a very human level, imaginatively projecting feelings of guilt, shame, reproach, reprimand – as though the scene were being enacted before our eyes.

Narrative (story-telling) intent such as that in Plate 6 fosters pictorial realism because it seeks to *convince* the beholder of the artist's vision of the circumstances of the event pictured, rather than merely to present effective or lucid images. We might say that true narrative art seeks to make us forget (at least momentarily) that we are looking at a work of art and seeks to evoke from us the reactions we would have had in witnessing the actual event depicted. In iconic art, by contrast, a realistic treatment of space and form is not required.

Iconic imagery must preserve and repeat those features of the prototype (i.e. of the original subject) which are important within the context in which the prototype is represented. The unambiguous representation of *distinction* (e.g. the ruler from the ruled, the blessed from the damned, etc.) is more important to this kind of imagery than any accurate imitation of elements of the visible ('real') world.

Narrative imagery is concerned with representing the 'how', 'when' and 'what' of events. It must provide clues enabling the beholder imaginatively to recreate an entire situation. Narrative imagery thus requires convincing ('realistic') formulae for depicting the setting of an event, the actions, interactions and intentions of the actors. These become even more important than distinctive individual features. It is apparent, therefore, that these two sub-divisions within the broad category of religious art, the iconic and the narrative, require very different treatments of formal elements, in accordance with the different kinds of meaning (story and symbol) and function which they generate and fulfil.

3 FROM CIRCA 1500 TO THE PRESENT: PUBLIC AND PRIVATE IMAGERY

Because the generic range (i.e. range of subject-matter) of medieval art was so limited, the distinction between iconic and narrative imagery seems adequate for categorizing art in the period *c.*400–*c.*1500 if our aim is to survey the broad sweep of Western art. (As already suggested, it would be an inadequate scheme of classification for the detailed study of medieval art.) But this distinction, albeit perennial, serves us less well in the period from *c.*1500 to the present. There are two main reasons for this: the increasing tendency of art to seek a faithful imitation of the real or visible world, even in iconic images, and the proliferation of the genres.

Both of these trends can, broadly speaking, be traced to the repopulation of Europe and the revival of urban civilization. As the rigid feudal hierarchy based on land tenure and military service was loosened, and retreat to isolated monastic communities no longer seemed the only sure route to salvation, so the artisans, merchants and professional people congregating in cities sought new models of order and piety. In order to keep its hold over such people, the church had to modify its approach. To this end the new preaching orders, the Franciscans and Dominicans who ministered to the urban population, began to place less emphasis on the transcendental and authoritarian aspects of Christian belief, and to stress its humanity. They preached the joys and sufferings of Jesus's life on earth, and the sentiments and tribulations of the Holy Family – Jesus, Mary and Joseph – the model of earthly families. In following the example of holy personages – the humble carpenter, the loving mother, the pious son – the secular activities of earning a livelihood, marrying, bringing up children, accumulating and disposing of wordly goods, could be made to seem compatible with Christian values.

In support of this new ethos, religious art increasingly either abandoned or softened the conventions of iconic imagery, so useful for evoking awe and veneration, in favour of the greater realism of narrative art, inviting viewers to participate imaginatively in the Christian story – this tale of suffering and redemption which continued to unfold in the world and within time. Its protagonists, painted and sculpted in every church, now sought to elicit pity and repentance from every individual viewer, to appear as if mirroring each viewer's own life, in order to guide all viewers' everyday behaviour.

It is a mistake to think of art as becoming secularized (i.e. concerned with the affairs of this world rather than with the sacred) in the Renaissance: the majority of images continued to depict religious subjects. Nevertheless, the uses of art broadened considerably beyond the church and the requirements of private devotion. Burgeoning lay institutions fostered the rise of new images, not necessarily strictly secular but calculated to foster community spirit, whether at the civic level or at the corporate level of craft and benevolent associations. Guild halls, government buildings, streets and town squares all began to acquire special forms of decoration. Rising prosperity now also enabled private citizens to embellish their homes, to express their aesthetic preferences at an individual level. A particular achievement of Western art at this time was the rise of portraiture, emphasizing the importance of the individual in both public and private contexts. In the exercise below on the poster and the miniature (pp.43–5) we shall gain an insight into the differing demands of these two types of imagery, the public and the private. It is this distinction which will help us broadly to categorize art from *c.*1500 to the present.

By *public art* is meant that which is intended for public viewing, whether commissioned and paid for by public bodies or by individuals or single families. By *private art* is meant art intended primarily for private viewing, whether in the home or in, for example, a private chapel. *Public* and *private* are not *genres,* or categories of subject-matter. They relate to the intended audience and environment of a work of art and, as such, can assist us further in our attempts to derive meaning from art. Within the genre of portraiture, for example, there are both private and public portraits which use the elements of painting in quite different ways in order to generate different meanings.

Exercise

Please try to imagine, and write down briefly, what your intentions and procedures might be if you decided to paint a miniature portrait of someone dear to you, perhaps to wear in a locket as a keepsake. Compare the demands that the subject-matter and intended recipient of such a work would make on you, and how you might respond, with the requirements of another undertaking: to design a large election poster portrait of a Prime Minister.

Don't worry if you have never drawn or painted a portrait, and don't get bogged down in the technicalities of tools and materials, or in the mechanics of capturing a resemblance. You are asked to use your imagination in a different direction: to introduce you to the way in which the function, subject-matter and intended recipient(s) of a work of art affect its final appearance. While both tasks fall within the broad genre or category of portraiture, they are at opposite ends of the private–public scale. Although photographs have today largely replaced painted miniatures, and election posters as such were unknown before the rise of electoral systems of government, both kinds of portraits, small private images and large public ones, are perennial types widely current in Western art.

Discussion

Don't expect to have covered all these points, but you should have included some of the following ideas.

Scale. The function and intended audience of each of these images dictates their size. By definition, a miniature is quite small, designed to be looked at by one person at a time, to be held in the hand and close to the eye. The poster needs to be large to be visible, to make an impact on many people simultaneously. Where the miniature encourages prolonged scrutiny, the poster must yield its message rapidly. Scale in turn influences the application of colours: small, delicate strokes in the miniature, large bold patches or heavy lines in the poster – these differences insure accord between the whole and the details, and reinforce the points already made about visibility and impact.

Colour. The same considerations would affect the choice of colours, regardless of the actual pigments or types of paint or ink, etc. used. You would probably resort to a quite different tonal range, and select different hues, for the miniature and the poster. (Remember: tone indicates that property of colour which makes it light or dark; *tonal range* means the 'distance' between the lightest and the darkest colour. *Hue* is that attribute in respect of which we speak of colour as red, blue, yellow, etc.) Rapid arousal of viewers, mobilizing their attention, enthusiasm, and allegiance all the way to the polling booth, is as much part of the function of a poster as ready visibility. In conjunction with size, this requirement tends to dictate the choice of a few bold, and boldly contrasting, colours. Too many different hues, a narrow or subtly graduated tonal range, might impede quick recognition of the image and dilute its impact. The natural colouring of the subject need not necessarily limit the artist's choice. Since colour is such an important vehicle for rapidly conveying meaning, one might wish to replace flesh, hair and eye colour with, for example, the red, white and blue of the British flag, to summon up at a glance all the associations viewers might be expected to have with this symbol of national unity and patriotism. A caption – the Prime Minister's name, a party slogan, an exhortation to vote – will help to get the message across. It is partly because of this use of verbal captions that we do not expect posters to be naturalistic representations (faithful imitations) of the world as we see it.

The miniature presents different problems. Recording the natural appearance of a subject is obviously important, since a major function of the image is to conjure up a likeness before the viewer's eye; you would probably wish to respect the sitter's actual colouring. The picture can be built up in quite subtle tonal gradations from dark to light, and in a wide range of hues to approximate the exact shade of the sitter's hair or skin, since the viewer can be relied upon to take time to 'read' it in all its details. Yet the aim of the miniature painter cannot be summed up simply as that of producing 'fidelity to natural appearances'. A miniature worn in a locket is a piece of jewellery. The locket or frame itself is usually made of a precious metal, and frequently adorned with precious or semi-precious stones or coloured enamels. The artist must ensure that the portrait is not entirely out of keeping with the mount and is not eclipsed by it. To this end, you would try to balance the record of the sitter's face with decorative values. Actual decoration might be added in the details of dress or background; most importantly, however, the decorative potential of colour could be used. The blue of a sitter's eye might be exaggerated, or dark irises lent additional lustre; jewel-like colour harmonies might be stressed. Muddy colour is unlikely to please in the miniature, and the earliest practitioners of the art even avoided the use of shadow modelling (using shade or shadow to indicate three-dimensionality or spatial qualities) altogether, preferring to indicate the roundness of the cheek, etc. through bright, sunlit hues only.

Likeness. 'Capturing a likeness' is usually thought to be the main, or even the only, intention of the portrait. We have already seen, however, different ways in which this aim may be modified to fulfil the particular function of specialized types of portraiture. Nevertheless, the problem of likeness remains, and you should have jotted down some ideas of the kind of likeness called for in the miniature and in the poster.

The intimate nature of the miniature seems to dictate a special kind of likeness, a private as opposed to a public face. You might strive to represent a characteristic expression of the sitter, perhaps a particularly lively or loving glance (a 'speaking likeness'), or to give a sense of the entire range or potential expressions of the sitter's face ('character'). The Elizabethan miniaturist Nicholas Hilliard (*c.*1547–1619) wrote that the limner (miniature specialist) must watch out for, and capture '... these lovely graces, witty smilings, and these stolen glances which suddenly, like lightening, pass and another countenance taketh place ...' (Hilliard, *Arte of Limning*, II. 23–4; the spelling has been simplified). The passage not only expresses the intentions of the artist, but gives us an insight into acceptable aristocratic modes of behaviour in Hilliard's age.

A large election poster, on the other hand (or any other very public likeness) is unlikely to be required to depict intimate qualities, or even a total personality. To make its point – that is the sitter is the best possible candidate for office – it might well seek to falsify genuine personal characteristics, investing the subject with the stereotypic qualities of an ideal Prime Minister, as enunciated in party propaganda or felt to be generally agreed by voters. Thus a weak politician might be made to show steely statesman-like determination – by striking up a pose exemplifying this quality in our culture – or an opportunist party hack might be lent an air of far-seeing wisdom. The sitter's actual features might even be subtly distorted to resemble a symbolic being, the British bull-dog for example, in analogy with the poster's colours. Formal devices are important means to these various ends. A low viewpoint – drawing the sitter as if seen from below – forces the viewer to 'look up to' the image, and may justify the subject's jaw protruding in an aggressive manner. Lighting can be directed and focused to give a 'sparkle' to the sitter's eye, or used to silhouette the candidate's profile, say, against the suggestion of a new dawn. These and many other such devices have all been used in drawn and photographic posters, and have become well-known clichés of what we might call a poster style. They almost all derive from the tricks originally devised by painters to portray rulers and other powerful personages in the heyday of 'state' portraiture (as the large-scale public portrait was called) in the sixteenth and seventeenth centuries. It is evident, from such observations, that there is a necessary and powerful connection between the function of a work of art, the way in which it is made or painted, and the meaning(s) it generates.

As we can see from this exercise, the demands of a given genre interact with those of the function of a work of art in order to set up certain expectations, govern the kinds of questions asked, affect the choice of medium and technique, and thereby the 'code' (of light, shape and colour) into which perception must be translated. Whatever the genre, or category of subject-matter, of the work we are considering, its public or private function plays a crucial role in the construction of its meaning. Further attention to these functions will be necessary before we resume our historical survey of genres.

3.1 PUBLIC ART

It should now be possible to go beyond the exercise on the poster and the miniature and think more generally about public and private art forms. Let us first of all list the requirements and characteristics of all or most public art. For example, we will think of the stylistic requirements of public art in general, and also raise the question of the degree of iconic or narrative treatment appropriate to public art. The aim of this discussion is not only to sharpen your ideas about the distinction between public and private art, but also, once again, to drawn your attention to the ways in which the intended functions or roles of works of art affect all aspects of artistic creation. When you have read these general points you will be asked to jot down briefly examples of public art visible today.

In listing the requirements or characteristics of all or most public art, we must consider the following.

Location. By definition, all public art must be at least potentially visible to the public. This is not as trivial a point as it may seem. Interpretation may hinge on it. For example, some art historians have ascribed public functions, such as political propaganda (to be treated presently) to works of art which were originally located in entirely private spaces. The chances are that such interpretations of a work's original meaning(s) are wrong.

Scale. Again, by definition, public art will tend to be large. Of course, details of large complexes may themselves be relatively small – such as the carvings on the capitals of columns in Gothic churches. Or discrete objects within larger entities may be small – church plate, for instance. But in general, when the work of art as a whole is meant to be visible to many, whether it be painting, sculpture or architecture, it will be large rather than small, and strive for bold effects.

Style (i.e. the way in which formal elements are characteristically handled by a particular artist or group of artists). This is a tricky area. In earlier periods, it is unlikely that a work intended to be seen by, and project a message to, large numbers of people, would have been used *primarily* as a vehicle for demonstrating an individual artist's personal style. But there are exceptions, notably in architecture. Plate 8 in your *Illustration booklet* reproduces a photograph of the church of Sant'Ivo della Sapienza (Saint Ivo of Wisdom), Rome, begun in 1642, to the design of the architect Borromini (1599–1667). Sant'Ivo is the chapel of the University of Rome; its entrance is at the apex of the semi-oval cloisters flanking the university buildings. While the lower part of the building harmonizes with the arcade of the cloisters, erected in the later part of the sixteenth century and designed by other architects, the tower-like lantern on top of the dome fully demonstrates Borromini's idiosyncratic fantastical inventiveness: it culminates in a spiral ramp. Anyone at all familiar with Borromini's work would instantly recognize this structure as his. Yet it should be said that the fanciful personal style is justified iconographically: the lantern is meant to recall pictorial representations of the Tower of Babel. Starting as a symbol of human folly, by the sixteenth century the Tower of Babel had come to symbolize the tower of wisdom, signifying the knowledge of tongues given to the apostles at Pentecost. So Borromini's demonstration of his personal style is harnessed to the ends of a conventionally suitable symbolism. Perhaps the safest statement to make about style and public art is that public art fosters a rather declamatory style, that is, one geared to evoke strong responses from the maximum number of viewers.

Iconicity. In general, public art is intended to arouse feelings of *community* among the viewers (worshippers, subjects, mourners). Iconic art was evolved primarily for public ends – embodying deities, celebrating rulers, commemorating the dead. Commonly, therefore public art fosters iconicity.

Exercise

After reading this general discussion, you might now like to list examples of categories of public art and architecture visible today. You should try to be logical in your response, perhaps distinguishing (as in the discussion below) between religious and secular functions, and starting out with large spaces or buildings before listing more detailed contents.

Discussion

You will notice that some of these categories are broader than others, and of a different type. All of the categories mentioned below come under the heading of public art, but there are subdivisions of function under this broad heading, which cuts across many kinds of subject-matter and art product.

Religious public art

Churches, or *synagogues*, or *mosques*, obviously, which are intended for public worship. Although some Christian denominations, and some other religions, avoid any kind of figurative decoration, others still rely on the repertory of *Christian art* codified in the Middle Ages. (Television programme 18 *The Victorian High Church* examines Victorian attitudes to church decoration.) In a Roman Catholic church, for example, we will find altarpieces, figures of saints, stained-glass windows representing episodes from the bible, etc. Cemeteries are often associated with church buildings. Many contain examples of *funerary memorial statuary*. Television programme 15 *Victorian Ways of Death* shows examples of Victorian funerary monuments.

Secular public art

Secular *public buildings*: government offices, the offices of large organizations dealing with, or catering to, the public, such as banks, insurance companies, airlines, etc. The termini of airlines and railways. Not only are such buildings often erected in a rather showy way, sometimes borrowing the styles associated with recognized 'artful' forms of architecture, such as Greek and Roman temples, but they are often adorned with *large murals* or *heroic sculptures* referring, either directly, through descriptive representations, or symbolically to the activities of the institutions for which they were commissioned. Such works may appear to us as propaganda: they are designed to foster a particular, and particularly favourable, view of the institution. Many court buildings, for example, are decorated with a sculpted allegorical figure of Justice: blindfolded to show that she is impartial, blind to differences of wealth or status between defendant and plaintiff; one hand holding the scales of fair judgment, the other the sword with which transgressors are punished. (If you have wondered why Justice is always female, that is because the personification accords with the feminine gender of the Latin word *Iustitia*. The same is true of personifications of Truth.) Not all symbolic and propagandizing figures take their form from medieval allegory like the figure of Justice. Outside the Trade Union Congress building in Great Russell Street, London, *The Spirit of Trade Unionism* is symbolized in a sculpture by Bernard Meadows representing two male figures, one of whom is struggling fraternally to raise the other, who has fallen to the ground.

Streets and squares, and especially parks, contain *memorials to statesmen, rulers, philanthropists, the war dead*. Television programme 10 *The Albert Memorial* explores the memorial erected to Prince Albert in Kensington Gardens. Some commemorative statuary forms a special category with its own traditions. The *equestrian monument* is a notable case in point. Plate 9 reproduces a photograph of an eighteenth-century *equestrian monument* to Peter the Great executed in Russia by the French sculptor Falconet at the behest of the Empress Catherine II. The tradition of such monuments goes back to ancient Rome, and was revived in the Renaissance. Falconet achieved what Leonardo da Vinci dreamt of in the 1490s but was technically unable to bring to completion: a huge bronze horse entirely supported on its hind legs.

3.2 AN EXAMPLE OF PUBLIC STATUARY: BERNINI'S *TRITON* FOUNTAIN

Had you thought of another sculptural type often encountered in city squares and parks: the fountain? The original function of fountains was to provide drinking and washing water to the inhabitants of cities, but they soon acquired symbolic connotations and by the Renaissance they were recognized as a specialized type of art product. Their symbolism in cities often refers to ideas of civic co-operation (necessary to complete the complex civil engineering required) and civic beneficence. When erected by individual benefactors, they may symbolize the munificence and status of the patron. And of course witty artists try to include some aquatic references also. Let's look at a particularly complex and famous example: Bernini's *Triton* fountain in Rome (Colour plate 3), erected in 1642–3 in the Piazza Barberini adjoining the Barberini palace built for the family of Pope Urban VIII Barberini. This seventeenth-century fountain is virtually an object lesson in how meaning is structured through the images and formal elements which constitute a work, and also in how multi-layered a work of art can be. Please attend particularly carefully to this example, checking the following discussion against the photograph reproduced in Colour Plate 3. (Remember that a photograph taken from a single viewpoint can never begin to do justice to a sculpture meant to be viewed in the round.) You will not be expected to remember the details of this discussion, simply to note the kinds of complexities which the careful reading of public imagery may entail.

Four dolphins rear up in the centre of a pool. Their joined tails fan out, supporting a large scallop-like shell. On the shell sits Triton, a sea divinity of ancient mythology, half man, half fish, son of Neptune, god of the Sea. He is blowing a conch (shell), out of which rises a jet of water.

The most widely read compilation of Graeco-Roman myth was, and is, the *Metamorphoses*, by the Latin poet Ovid (43 BC–16 AD). Until recently, it was standard literary fare for all educated people, and a source book for artists. We should not therefore be surprised to find a description by Ovid of the scene depicted by Bernini. 'After the Flood', he writes,

> [...Neptune] lays by his three-pronged spear and calms the waves; and, calling sea-hued Triton, showing forth above the deep, his shoulders thick o'ergrown with shell-fish, he bids him blow into his loud-resounding conch, and by that signal to recall the floods and streams. He lifts his hollow, twisted shell, which grows from the least and lowest to a broad swelling whorl. [...] So then, when it had touched the sea-god's lips wet with his dripping beard, and sounded forth the retreat which had been ordered, 'twas heard by all the waters both of land and sea; and all the waters by which 'twas heard it held in check. Now the sea has shores, the rivers, bank full, keep within their channels; the floods subside. [...] (Ovid, *Metamorphoses*, Book I, lines 330–44)

A fairly naive observer will have understood, seeing the dolphins, the shells, and the half-fishy naked creature, that the fountain's imagery refers to a watery realm. But a better read viewer, recalling Ovid, will know that the fountain represents waters commanded to 'keep within their channels', beneficent waters in contrast to the destructive water of the Flood.

There is more, however. In the fashionable 'emblem books' of the seventeenth century, an adult form of picture book, authors and artists compiled series of images whose symbolic significance was amplified by mottoes and text. Some of these images were family crests, others supposedly of universal application. In the emblem books, Triton was an emblem of 'Immortality acquired by literary study' – don't ask why! Thus a viewer who was not only well-educated, but also *au fait* with the emblematic literature, might suspect that this meaning was intended to enrich the significance of the fountain. Such a viewer would be well aware, from the location of the fountain near the Barberini palace and the coat of arms of Pope Urban VIII Barberini prominently displayed between the dolphins' tails, of the identity of the fountain's patron. Like all literate Romans, this viewer would also know that the Pope was an accomplished poet. Putting two and two together, our knowledgeable beholder would conclude that the emblematic meaning of Triton was a compliment to the poetic pope.

Urban VIII's coat of arms consists of an escutcheon with the Barberini bees, surmounted by the papal triple crown and backed with the crossed keys of Saint Peter, symbol of the pope's authority as Vicar of Christ in direct line from Saint Peter. It is perfectly standard to display a patron's coat of arms on a public monument, but in this case the armorial bearings add a further meaning to the fountain. Bernini has emphasized the gigantic bees, carving them to look like living insects crawling on the shield. Bees, who give mankind sweet honey, were a recognized emblem of divine providence. Finally, the dolphins, so suitable a base for the sea god Triton, also had an emblematic significance. They symbolized princely benefaction.

In the curious habits of thought of the seventeenth century, which sought symbolic meaning in the phenomena of the natural world, the *Triton* fountain thus expressed ideas of divine and princely benefaction, extolled the talents as well as the munificence of the patron, and exemplified aquatic imagery in the cultivated idiom of Graeco-Roman mythology. But it is not very important that every seventeenth-century viewer, and even fewer twentieth-century viewers, derive all these precise meanings from Bernini's sculpture. What is important is that each layer of symbolism reinforces and enriches the primary meaning of the fountain: channelling cleansing, refreshing, cooling waters into the heart of the city, recalling a world of natural elements subjected to the beneficent operations of human artifice. Bernini's fountain beautifully fulfils its functions. Notice (if you can see it in our reproduction) the way the jet of water from Triton's conch bathes his naked torso, streams down into the scallop shell, spills over the sides of the shell into the basin below. It is an apt and arresting image, playful and solemn at the same time, a near-perfect example of public art.

If this discussion has focused on sculpture, that is because sculpture is the pre-eminent medium of public art. It complements architecture in the way in which it helps to organize municipal space – think for example of the way a three-dimensional sculpture can mark a cross-roads; now think of a two-dimensional painting in the same location. Sculpture is not as dependent as painting or mosaic on pre-existing architecture (that is, you need a *wall* on which to paint a mural or execute a mosaic), yet it can be used to ornament architecture. Above all, sculpture is durable. When made in the right medium, such as bronze which withstands all weathers, sculpture can be permanently placed outdoors, where it can be seen by everyone. Large sculpture is too heavy to be stolen, and relatively vandal proof. Very expensive, it requires much lengthy collaborative effort to produce; it is thus an excellent testimonial to corporate or state patronage. But despite the weight given to sculpture in this treatment of public art, you should recall that other media, such as mural painting and mosaic, lend themselves equally, or nearly equally well to public functions.

3.3 SOME TWENTIETH-CENTURY REACTIONS TO THE TRADITIONS OF PUBLIC ART

Exercise

Just as the traditional boundaries and content of the category *art* have been challenged by twentieth-century artists, so our traditional notions of the aims and uses of *public* art have come under fire, to the frequent indignation of the general public. In order to make sense of these developments, however, it is important to understand what it is that artists are reacting against. Each category of art arouses, through the history of its conventions, certain expectations in the viewer. This is true of the broad category, *public art*. So let us make explicit what those who commissioned public monuments in the past, or who commission traditional types of public art today, have hoped to achieve or to express. Please try to summarize now, not the types and characteristic problems of public art, but, at the broadest possible level, its traditional aims. Briefly list your ideas before reading the discussion below.

Discussion

In general, by appealing to a wide audience, public art has aimed to *reinforce* or to *forge communal attitudes. Durable* public monuments have been designed to pre-empt the judgements of history, that is, to impose a certain outlook not only on contemporaries but also on future generations.

Let's take an imaginary example. A usurper captures the throne of Ruritania. He immediately commissions vast numbers of monuments depicting him in the various iconic poses associated with hereditary monarchy and the exercise of royal power: seated on the throne, crowned and holding sceptre and orb; commanding his troops; dispensing justice and charity; receiving tribute, etc. He may have himself portrayed with his wife and eldest son, to demonstrate his dynastic aspirations: the orderly devolution of kingship from himself to his heir.

Through all these monuments he hopes to: *reinforce* Ruritanian traditions of loyalty to the crown, *forge* new bonds, of allegiance, respect, fear, admiration, etc., between himself and his subjects; convince future generations of Ruritanians that his rule was successful and thus legitimate. He may even order monumental portraits of earlier kings to be defaced or modified to bear his own features, hoping thereby to *alter collective memory*.

This example is schematic and imaginary, but there have been countless instances just like it throughout European history, from ancient Egypt to ancient Rome, to Imperial Russia, Napoleonic France, and in many other societies. The Albert Memorial, which is the subject of Television programme 10, is an analogous example from Victorian Britain, attempting to present the image of Prince Albert as a patron of art and sciences, and as an example of virtue.

From the late nineteenth century onwards, public art has consistently proclaimed the importance, the overwhelming value, of *communal attitudes* and *social life*. (Ford Madox Brown's murals in Manchester Town Hall are an example considered later in the course.) Of course, public art has not always been used to project ideal relations between a ruler and his subjects as in our Ruritanian example. Communal attitudes most often expressed through public art in the past have included: *the affirmation of allegiance to, and pride in, collective identity*. Equally important in public art has been the affirmation of *collective values or ideals* (for instance, loyalty, justice, charity, courage, etc.). Public art has also attempted to arouse in its viewers the *desire to emulate actions best exemplifying collective values or ideas* (the courage of soldiers who have died in defence of their country, the fraternal behaviour of unionists, the philanthropy of public benefactors, etc.). It has often been used to evoke *awe of the divine and of its earthly manifestations*.

Twentieth-century challenges to the traditional aims of public art have taken many forms. One of the most complex is that of *Performance Art*. Instead of making an enduring monument, the artist performs, or causes to be performed, some public action or sequence of actions, the course of which may be affected by the reaction of 'viewers'. The latter may even be unaware, at least initially, that they are participating in an *art* event. A 'Performance', 'Environment' or 'Happening' (one such 'happening', of a kind common in the 1960s, involved the artist spending a week shut in a gym-locker with a urine-bottle and labelling the product of the ordeal 'a duration-confinement-body-piece') thus subverts the traditional roles of artist, monument and viewers, blurring the distinctions between them, and indeed the distinctions between *art* and 'life'. If the artist's actions are, as they often are in this type of presentation, enigmatic – that is, unclear in intent or significance, even 'meaningless' – or counter to acceptable norms of social behaviour, the possibility of evoking a *collective* response is expressly denied. On the contrary, a *fragmentation* of audience response is almost certainly ensured. Viewers will be forced to become aware of *individual differences* amongst themselves through their different reactions to or interpretations of the artist's performance. They may even be led to think about the problematic nature of *meaning*, the difficulties of communication, the unforeseen consequences of actions and the way context influences our reading of events. All of this is in contrast to the seeming clarity of shared significance, the enduring messages, of traditional public art.

Land Art and *Impossible Art* are names of a somewhat different kind of statement collectively characterized as *Eccentric Action*. Transient marks, usually on a gigantic scale, are made on the earth's surface: a field is ploughed or seeded to form unusual patterns, trenches are dug in the desert, a path is worn in virgin territory, the frozen surface of a river is cut into, huge but fragile earthworks erected. (Perhaps the chalkland marking of pre-historic people, like the Cerne Abbas Giant, inspired some of these gestures.) The Bulgarian-born American artist Christo (b. 1935) 'packages' buildings and coastlines, wrapping them in polythene or canvas. Some of these projects are intended to be seen only in the form of plans or 'ideas' – concepts, hence *Conceptual Art*. But others have been executed (Plate 10). Huge as the pyramids, but ephemeral, serving no practical purpose, glorifying no one, works such as these also subvert traditional notions of public art. Instead of proclaiming the supreme importance of social life and collective values, they usually represent quirks of the individual imagination. Far from attempting to pre-empt the judgment of history, they can even be read as metaphors of the *insignificance* of human history vis-à-vis Nature, or Time, or the Planet Earth.

Much of the grandly subversive point of these artistic gestures, however, is lost through the way in which they must be recorded in order to enter the art market and, for that matter, the history of art. Plate 10 reproduces, of course, a photograph; Land Artists also exhibit and sell plans and sketches of their unrealized projects. Happenings, Environments and Performances too are enshrined in photographs or on film. By thus being given permanent shape, these ephemeral and polemical events are reduced to small-scale, marketable commodities, and find a place in galleries, museums and private collections in exactly the way in which easel paintings do.

An artist who is fully aware of the complexities and paradoxes of public art and indeed exploits them is the Swedish-born American sculptor and draftsman Claes Oldenberg (b. 1929). He has deliberately utilized exhibitions to explore various themes through drawings and three-dimensional works brought together for the occasion, and which could not otherwise have been seen altogether. He makes use of the contrast between our sense of the frivolous (small-scale) and the grandiose (large-scale), the ephemeral and the enduring, the domestic and the monumental. In 1965 he exhibited the first of a series of drawings of imaginary, or 'projected' colossal monuments for actual locations. Plates 11 and 12 are two examples from this series. Plate 11 reproduces a tourist postcard of the Thames with a view of the Palace of Westminster. On it Oldenburg has drawn two ballcocks, floating on the river. In this context the homely objects, normally housed in lavatory cisterns, arouse curious associations, from the ridiculous to the serious. Is Oldenburg 'stating' that the Thames is no more important or 'noble' than a flush lavatory, ready to be emptied at the flick of some gigantic hand? Do the ballcocks 'celebrate' the engineering genius of the British, inventors of the flush lavatory? Is he making fun of the grandiose traditions of public monuments, or is he bemoaning the state of modern urban civilization, in which nothing more elevated than sanitary expertise remains to be commemorated?

Plate 12 is more typical of the rest of the series in that it is entirely drawn by the artist. The prospect of Park Avenue, the poshest residential street in New York, straight as an arrow and flanked with luxurious blocks of flats, is blocked with a colossal 'Good Humor' bar – chocolate-covered vanilla ice cream on a stick, a popular American children's sweet. A corner of it has been bitten off, providing a pedestrian passage, and the bar, crammed down between the houses, seems to be just beginning to melt.

Here are some statements by Oldenburg that are relevant. In 1965 he had just returned to New York, to a loft of enormous proportions:

> The 'monument' drawings beginning at this time were stimulated by the new scale and also by the viewpoint from an airplane. The area in which the objects are placed grows from a room to a landscape, like that shown on a postcard. The objects consequently become 'colossal', since the landscape, being a real one, cannot be taken as a miniature. A large part of the pleasure of drawing is the awareness of shifting scale. One effect of the monument drawings is an imaginary expansion of the drawing scale.

The theme of scale is elaborated in Oldenburg's 'Introduction' to his Tate Gallery exhibition in 1970:

> I have always been fascinated by the values attached to size. Aside from the technical accomplishments involved, why is a four hundred foot high clothes-pin more valuable than one I can hold in my hand? Also – considerations of size are a way to ask into the reality of vision; what is perspective, and is size completely subject to the will. The first 'monument' drawings were like stereoptic combines of two viewpoints – a small thing viewed close seeming 'colossal' because of its super-imposition on a large thing viewed from afar.

The subject-matter of his work, Oldenburg's writes, is 'city nature':

> City nature is made up of streets, houses, stores, advertisements, makeup, clothing and vehicles. Makeup and clothing & the people who animate them are like trees, vehicles like animals. Stores are forests, streets plains and rivers, advertisements and goods so many creeping and crawling dreams.
> [...] What kind of nature is city nature. It's a piece of man's mind. To live in the city is to live inside oneself.

In another context, he speaks of the '[...] irrationality, disconnection, violence and stunted expression – the damaged life forces of the city street'.

Perhaps the most poetical and evocative of Oldenburg's projected monuments is his model for a *Feasible Monument for a City Square: Hats Blowing in the Wind*, now appropriately housed in a private collection in Chicago, the 'Windy City' (Colour Plate 4). By identifying the human scale with the tiny wire figures on the base, we perceive the hats as colossal. These man-made accessories, clothing for everyday use, shabby, non-durable, objects of 'city nature' – blown off in the whirlwinds at the foot of tall buildings, in the canyons of American city streets – recall the loneliness of walking anonymously through large cities; these *hats* – how mysterious, how terrifying it would be really to move through a forest of huge, precariously poised, monumentally enduring, *bronze hats*!

Another way of thinking about Oldenburg's imaginary monuments is that he conflates, in these drawings and models, notions of domestic or private art (to be treated presently), such as *still life* and *landscape*, with notions of public art, monumental sculpture. Because our culture has made us quite sensitive to the traditional differences between these categories, the seeming juxtaposition of the two within one visual field has the power to startle us, to make us laugh and to make us think.

These works have been discussed not only in order to illustrate some twentieth-century art products with which you may be unfamiliar, but also to point out yet again the way in which *how* we categorize or classify our world itself generates and transforms meaning. On page 16 we queried whether the inscription *Keith Arnatt Is an Artist* written on a public lavatory wall would have the same significance for us that it has on the wall of an art gallery or reproduced in a text on the history of art. Duchamp's *Fontaine* plays on the same theme: calling into question the traditional boundaries between our categories of *art* and non-art. Oldenburg's imaginary monuments not only take up the same topic but also challenge or confound our expectations of different categories *within* art. Their capacity to stimulate meaning depends directly on expectations we may not have known we had.

If you have previously thought that meaning in art derives mainly from subject-matter, and the emotional, literary or historical associations we all bring to subject-matter (mother and child = maternal love; a pretty landscape = memories of a summer day, love of nature; Battle of Waterloo = British victory, defeat of Napoleon), you should begin to question and perhaps revise your ideas. The significance, the 'value', of a clothes-peg in the hand is not the same as that of a clothes-peg four-hundred feet high (Plate 13). The drawing reproduced in Plate 13 stimulates meaning because, small though it is, it makes us think that we see a clothes-peg four hundred feet high. It does so by borrowing methods of representation associated with depicting a colossal scale, and we expect that scale in turn to be reserved for important public statements, for the evocation of valuable communal attitudes, the affirmation of communal ideals.

Exercise

Before we move on to discuss the categories of private or domestic art, it would be useful to analyse Plate 13 to discover by what means, what methods of representation, Oldenburg suggests the colossal size of the clothes-peg. Ask yourself: where is my viewpoint (that is, where would I stand in order to see the clothes-peg as it appears in the drawing)? What is the function of the base line at the foot of the clothes-peg? Of the slightly splayed legs of the clothes-peg? Of the shading?

Discussion

You probably noticed that Oldenburg has used perspective to persuade us that we view the clothes-peg from below. (We can see its underside, between the legs, not the top surface as we could if we were looking down on it.) Since we know the human scale intimately, we 'deduce' that the peg is large enough to permit us to stand at its feet, looking up. The base line then resembles the ground, not a table top. The legs are splayed to increase the sense of height: the steeper the angle at which the width of the peg is seen to diminish, the sharper our sense of perspectival recession (think of railway lines meeting at a point on the horizon), and thus the higher does the top of the peg seem. The shading suggests the effects of sunlight, increasing our sense of viewing the peg outdoors. In fact, as the title suggests, Oldenburg has drawn the humble clothes-peg as he might have drawn a skyscraper.

In fact, Oldenburg's *Clothespin* was erected, at a height of 45 ft (13.75m), at a site in Philadelphia. Not only does the construction of the *Clothespin* as a monument derive meaning from the way in which it defeats our expectations of public art, but also in its references to and associations with other factors both internal and external to the world of art. Here is what Robert Hughes, a modern art critic, says of the monument:

> It represents the Magrittean experience of the giant apple in the room, or the magically enlarged comb leaning over the diminutive bed, but puts it into a real city. At the same time, the clothes-pin is not simply that. Its jaws, facing one another and bound together by the spring-clip, refer to Brancusi's embracing lovers, fused into one mass of cubical stone; while the whole clothes-pin has two legs, and so encourages one to read it as an effigy of man. The spring-clip on its 'torso', magnified and gleaming against the rust, suggests compression, force, military inhibition. All the angles are sharp. It is an authority figure, a parody of the Hero in sculpture – in fact, a modern Colossus of Rhodes, supplying Oldenburg's alternative to the classical tradition of monumental sculpture, once mordantly summed up by him as 'bulls and greek and nekkid broads'. (R. Hughes, *The Shock of the New,* p.359)

This is not to say that all twentieth-century public art subverts, rather than reinforces, the proclamation of communal attitudes. The great ceramic walls created by Miró at the UNESCO building in Paris (1958) and Picasso's *Guernica* testify to this, as do the many war memorials offered to our scrutiny. As with other aspects of art, however, the different meanings we derive from all the works discussed in this section are influenced by our knowledge of the traditions of public art at different times and in different places.

4 PRIVATE OR DOMESTIC ART

The fifteenth century (see above, pp.35–6), saw an explosion not only in the public uses of art but also in the private, domestic functions of imagery. A detailed discussion of some of the types of private art evolved in the Early Renaissance properly belongs in a Renaissance art course (see A353, *Art in Fifteenth-Century Italy*): some specialized forms such as the *deschi da parto* ('birth trays') or *cassoni* (painted chests and furniture panels), are of importance mainly in their own period. Although many such furnishings perished, some have survived. Wrested out of their original domestic contexts, they have entered museums as framed easel pictures – thus rather falsifying our sense of the evolution of portable easel painting by making us think that this form of art emerged earlier than in fact it did. See for example illustration 107 in *Art and Illusion*. This was originally probably part of a panelling frieze rather than an independent scene, which is how it is now displayed in the Ashmolean Museum, Oxford. The fifteenth century also saw a revival of small-scale bronze sculpture, both in three dimensions and in relief. Such works were sometimes based on antique themes. But the best-known small-scale bronze reliefs of the early Renaissance were portrait medals. Bronze, of course, is an expensive medium, so the use of pieces like these was never as widespread as that of painted birth trays and decorated furniture. They were restricted to educated professional and aristocratic circles. Scholars, and those with pretensions to culture, would keep bronze statutettes on their desks. Sometimes these were functional, inkwells, lamps, little boxes (see illustration 81 in *Art and Illusion*). Medals would be exchanged with friends and sent to admirers or favoured clients. Princes could use them to reward deserving subjects. Although essentially an intimate art form – to be viewed, like the painted miniature, by one person at a time, held in the hand and appreciated for detailed execution as well as preciousness of material – small bronzes became, from the sixteenth century, a currency of international diplomacy. The genre, much debased, is perpetuated in the metal trophies and medals now given in competitions and in commemoration of specific events.

Other types of private art of the Renaissance, however, have endured and evolved in forms closer to their original. Private devotional imagery continues to be produced, both in cheap and in luxury forms – although the fifteenth-century woodcut has been replaced by photographic reproductions, and the carved, gilded and painted folding devotional 'altarpiece' is no longer made except as an imitation of medieval and Renaissance originals. Portraiture, of course, continues to be produced – although this, too, has changed in medium: photographs have ousted, in most households, the painted portrait or the portrait bust.

Most of the domestic or private art with which we are familiar, however, came into prominence not in the fifteenth but in the sixteenth century, with a change in the models of private collecting.

5 THE RISE AND INFLUENCE OF COLLECTING

Collecting, practised by ancient Greek and Roman magnates, was revived in the fifteenth century by such grandees as the Duke of Berry, uncle of the King of France, and Piero de' Medici, head of the great Florentine banking family and unofficial ruler of Florence.

Let us recall what is meant by collecting. All the appurtenances of a wealthy Renaissance household – *cassoni* and other furnishings, tapestries, tabernacles, silverware, jewellery, armour, elaborately tailored clothes in precious textiles, commemorative and celebratory portraits, illustrated books – did not in themselves constitute a collection, any more than did commissioned altarpieces and funerary monuments. To collect means to divest objects of their primary function – be it adornment, commemoration, an aid to devotion – and to value them for other reasons. The early collectors, such as the Duke of Berry and Piero de' Medici, prized the items in their collections for their rarity, for historical associations, such as those connected with ancient coins and medals, for the preciousness of their materials, and for the beauty of their workmanship. When Piero, called 'the Gouty', was incapacitated through his illness, he had

> [...] himself carried to his study [...] there he would look at his books as if they were a pile of gold. [...] One day he may simply want for his pleasure to let his eyes pass along these volumes to while away the time and give recreation to the eye. The next day, then [...] he takes out some of the effigies and images of all the Emperors and Worthies of the past, some made of gold, some of silver, some of bronze, of precious stones or of marble and other materials, which are wonderful to behold. Their worth is such that they give the greatest enjoyment and pleasure to the eye. The next day he would look at his jewels and precious stones [...] he takes great pleasure and delight in looking at those and in discussing their various powers and excellencies [as amulets]. The next day, maybe, he inspects his vases of gold and silver and other precious material and praises their noble worth and the skill of the masters who wrought them. All in all when it is a matter of acquiring worthy or strange objects he does not look at the price. (Filarete, *Treatise on Architecture* (c.1640s), cited in Gombrich, 'The early Medici as patrons of art', *Norm and Form*, p.51)

You will note that paintings are not mentioned. With the beginning of collecting paintings in the sixteenth century, which seems to have started in northern Italy, the criteria of rarity and preciousness, so important to fifteenth-century collectors, had to be revised. The works of certain artists were indeed few and difficult to obtain, but contemporary paintings in general – and there were really few others to be collected – were not rare and could indeed be produced on demand. The material costs of easel pictures could never match those of objects such as gems and gold and silver vases, although some paintings used expensive pigments or gold leaf, and very small pictures might be executed on a costly copper plate or even an ivory support. Beauty of workmanship became the overriding factor governing the collectable value of paintings, and the more discriminating a collector of pictures, the more did he or she come to disregard material costs for virtuosity of execution.

Workmanship, or execution, in painting is hardly separable from the treatment of visual form (colour, shape, space); the latter, in turn, is related to (albeit not necessarily dependent on) the subject represented. That is, it is difficult to judge the formal and technical treatment of a subject without comparing it both with other treatments of the same or similar subjects, and the subject itself, or a similar one, as it is perceived in reality.

It was, no doubt, subject-matter which first fuelled the interest in images, and indeed continues to do so for many people. Thus pious motifs, like those depicted in devotional imagery, were perhaps the first to be collected – not primarily as an aid to prayer, but as 'works of *art*'. Thinking of pious images mainly in terms of their power to evoke religious feelings tends to foster traditionalism: the nearer the image is to some revered precedent, familiar to the devout, the more authentic a likeness it seems of the holy personages, and the more worthy of veneration. This is the spirit animating the conservative Byzantine icons. The collector's interest, on the other hand, being in execution and the way in which formal elements are used to depict a particular subject, tends to encourage the artist's desire to outdo his predecessors, to innovate and to invent, both in the treatment of subject-matter and in subject-matter itself. Each genre carried its own *conventions*, 'rules', challenges, possibilities or problems, which would have been known to artists and collectors alike.

Let us focus our attention for a few pages on some private works utilizing the scheme of many Byzantine icons, the half-length Madonna and Child. Let us consider the series of smallish Madonna pictures by Raphael (1483–1520), executed between 1504 and *c.*1508 for connoisseurs and collectors. Raphael was not the first to employ the subject in an individualistic manner: fifteenth-century Florentine sculptors, notably Donatello (c.1386–1466) and his followers had paved the way through variations on the theme in reliefs for both domestic and public use (Plate 14). But Raphael was perhaps the first artist to use such a series largely as a means of artistic self-improvement. Having come to Florence from Umbria, steeped in the sweet but monotonous manner of his master Perugino, Raphael was overwhelmed by the achievements of the Florentines which he now saw about him. His Madonna pieces were a way of absorbing the many lessons of Florentine art, and making them his own. Not only the fifteenth-century works of Donatello and his followers, but also the current practice of his older Florentine contemporaries, notably Leonardo (1452–1519) and Michelangelo (1475–1564) (Plate 15) were grist to his mill. In drawing freely upon previous artistic achievements, and painting a series of variations on such a circumscribed theme, Raphael demonstrates in a particularly vivid way the *relative autonomy* of Renaissance art. (Recall the discussion of *relative autonomy* on pp.13–15.) The subject was attractive, ideally suited to domestic interiors, and of a type already found in most Florentine households. The rise of a well-to-do art-collecting public meant that innovation within this traditional scheme would be welcomed. Like the aims and rules of a chess game, the problems of the genre were well understood by artists and viewers alike. Any refinements would be noticed and appreciated. The modest scale and the limited number of 'pieces' in this particular game or sub-genre – one Madonna and her Child – also limited the difficulties, while admitting of infinite permutations.

Three of Raphael's half-length Madonna pictures are reproduced in your *Illustration booklet*: the *Solly Madonna*, now in Berlin; the *Tempi Madonna*, now in Munich; and the *Large Cowper Madonna*, now in Washington (Colour plates 5, 6 and 7). (The names by which these and other Raphael Madonnas are known are those of private collectors who owned the pictures before they entered national museums; they do not, however, identify the original owners.)

The *Solly Madonna*, *c.*1500, is the earliest of these pictures, dating from before Raphael's Florentine sojourn and the Florentine series of Madonnas. It exemplifies the artist's dependence on his teacher, Perugino. The *Tempi Madonna*, 1507–8, is one of the last paintings of this subject completed in Florence. The *Large Cowper Madonna*, dated by the artist 1508, may have been executed late in that year in Rome and sent back to Florence. At this time

Raphael was already engaged on large-scale mural paintings for the papal apartments in the Vatican palace.

Do not be put off by the many sentimental imitations and reproductions of these paintings, the souvenirs and chocolate boxes. These pictures are well worth analysing closely, and there is nothing philistine in enjoying their agreeable subject-matter and pleasing manner.

Exercise

Please look very closely at all three of the reproductions. Consider, first, the conventions or formulae employed by Raphael. What are the 'rules' of this 'game', that is, the choices available to the artist, the particular problems of the genre? Secondly, compare the three plates. Note first the overall compositional relationships, of the figures to the background, to the total picture space, and to the frame. It may help you to use a ruler or tape measure for this part of the exercise in order to work out the relative proportions of these elements. Then analyse any differences in the relationship of the figures to each other, in the poses of individual figures, in the way figures are structured.

The aim of this exercise is to compel you to discriminate between different treatments of the same subject and between the subject itself (a young mother and child, in this instance) and the formal elements used to represent or depict it. If only we could do this in front of the originals, you would be learning to look at pictures like a truly discerning collector, one who is not dazzled by preciousness of material or even market value, but attends to refinements of execution.

Discussion

You should not expect to have covered all the points in this discussion.

1 *The 'rules of the game'*. All three pictures are vertical rectangles, accommodating the half-length figure of the Virgin Mary, approximately three-quarter life size, and the full-length figure of the Christ Child, silhouetted against a background of landscape and/or sky. The Virgin is clothed and the Christ Child nearly naked. He resembles, like most Italian Renaissance depictions of the Christ Child or of child-like angels, a *putto* (plural *putti*), that naked chubby baby-like figure of ancient Graeco-Roman art, whose age was left rather vague, and who was capable of adult action beyond the capacity of real babies.

Have you asked yourself why this format – a half-length adult and a full-length baby – is so often employed, and seems so natural? If the actual difference of scale between adult and baby is to be respected, and the two are to be shown in close contact, then depicting the adult at full length must reduce the size of the child in the picture. That is, the representation of the child would then take up less of the picture surface. Within the normal proportions of an easel painting – the width just under three-quarters of the height – the size of the adult, were she represented at full-length, would also have to be reduced, and more of the picture surface taken up by 'background' on either side of the figure. Only on an exaggeratedly tall and thin panel, can a full-length adult figure take up so much of the picture surface. So if the artist wishes to place the figures 'close up' to the viewer, that is, taking up most of the foreground or of the picture surface (think of looking at something through a framed window), and to give prominence to a small child, he is really forced to reduce the proportion of the adult body shown from full-length to half-length or less.

The images in all three paintings are somewhere between *icon* and *narrative*. Although no specific moment is really indicated, nor even a particular location, the generalized gold-leaf ground of earlier Madonnas (with its association of unearthly radiance, non-measurable space, and royal magnificence) has been replaced by an earthly out-of-doors: a landscape, a cloudless sky, warm sunshine bathing the figures. The Mother and Child act and interact: attending to a book, clasped in an embrace, etc. And these specific actions, like all human actions, imply the passage of time. Insofar as the formula is *iconic*, what it depicts is not the status of the Virgin Mary as Queen of Heaven, and of the infant Jesus as divine: rather, it is an image of idyllic motherhood, an ideal relationship between a loving young mother and her baby. It is an icon particularly suited to a domestic situation, a family home. Insofar as it is *narrative*, the story represented is of a particular interaction between mother and child – but also of something else, which the viewer must bring to the image. Our knowledge of the Gospels prompts us to ask: does the Virgin, does the Child, know of the Passion which is to come? Are they aware, what do they think, of the role of Christ in the story of our Redemption? The narrative, in other words, suggests two kinds of time: a short moment, and the long history of humankind – the Creation, the Fall, the Incarnation, the Redemption. (The Incarnation, 'God made flesh', is the birth of Jesus as a human child of a human mother. Theologians speak of Mary as the 'instrument of the Incarnation', without whom there could be no Redemption, no salvation for humankind.)

These are some of the 'rules of the game' governing not only Raphael's paintings, but also most of the other Italian Renaissance domestic Madonnas, which form a small but discrete sub-genre under the broader heading of religious art.

2 *Variations*. I hope that when you compared Raphael's paintings, you noticed the different relationships of the figures to their background. In the *Solly* (Colour plate 5) and *Tempi* (Colour plate 6) *Madonnas* this is largely a function of the placing of the horizon line. The panel of the *Solly Madonna* has been 'divided' into three; the land occupies almost exactly two thirds of the height of the picture, and the sky one third. This means that we see the Madonna as if she were seated rather high above the ground (perhaps on a balcony – although Raphael does not give us any precise indications). Despite the fact that the Madonna and Child occupy all of the foreground, our attention is drawn to the incidents of landscape, notably the feathery little trees on the outcropping on our left. These delicate silhouettes were virtually a trademark of Raphael's master Perugino.

The horizon line is much lower in the *Tempi Madonna*. This panel seems to have been subdivided into fifths, the land occupying two-fifths, the sky three-fifths of the height of the picture (that is, it is one and a half times the height of the land-strip). This has two consequences. First, Mother and Child seem to be standing rather lower down, and even though the middleground is masked from view by the Virgin's swirling cloak, the figures seem rather better integrated with the landscape. Secondly, since so much more of the background is sky, there is less incident to distract us from the figures and their tender embrace.

Some of these effects of the horizon line may not be immediately clear to you. It is important to recall that, in nature, the line of the horizon is always directly related to the height of our eyes. That is why, when we stand high on a mountain, we see so much more of the countryside: the horizon is as high as we. When we sit on a flat beach, the horizon – the line between sea and sky – is quite low; it is dramatically heightened when we stand up, and even more if we climb on to a jetty of some other object above ground level (see Figure 5 above, on viewpoints). Thus, in the *Solly Madonna* we are made to feel that our eye level is only slightly below that of the Virgin – at her shoulder line, to be precise. We, like she, are 'placed' high above the countryside. In the *Tempi Madonna*, on the other hand, our eye level is rather lower down, roughly at the height at which the Virgin supports the Child with her left hand. The figures seem to loom slightly above us (rather as if we were kneeling in front of them). They seem better integrated with the landscape because we feel that (in contrast with the *Solly Madonna*) no great discrepancy of ground level intervenes between the foreground on which the figures are placed and the distant background. Although the Virgin is no longer 'enthroned' on high above the landscape, and the image itself is of great intimacy, our lowered viewpoint, with its suggestion of reverence, helps to distance the image from the everyday and gives it an air of solemnity.

You've probably noticed that in both the *Solly* and *Tempi Madonnas* the figure groups each form, roughly speaking, an isosceles triangle (a triangle with two equal sides). This is not the case in the *Large Cowper Madonna* (Colour plate 7) where the figures are inscribed in a trapezoid (a shape bounded by four straight lines of which no two are parallel). Because the silhouette of the figures does not taper as sharply as in Colour Plates 5 and 6, far less of the background is visible – and only a hard edge on the right-hand side of the picture demarcates sky from ... not so much *ground* as the back of the seat or the parapet of a balcony. Although this line, just below the middle of the panel, acts like the horizon in suggesting our eye level, it does not signify distance from foreground to background. The effect of these two devices, the trapezoid disposition of the figures and the shallowness of the picture space, is two-fold. The figures seem bulkier than those of the *Solly* and *Tempi Madonnas* and, since our view into depth is blocked, they seem even closer to us, as if thrust forward. This is furthered by the pose of the figures, to which I shall return presently.

3 *Relationships and poses.* You must have compared the actions of the Mother and Child in these paintings, their poses and physical types. Let us first discuss the poses. The *Solly Madonna* is seated parallel to the picture plane (again, it helps to think of the picture as a window and the picture plane as the window pane or a plane parallel to it). Head, torso and shoulders are aligned with the surface of the painting – we see the Virgin in full-face. The book in her foreshortened right hand serves to define the space between the 'front' of the picture and her shoulders. The pose of the Christ Child on her lap is slightly more complicated. His body is at an angle to the picture plane – his left shoulder drawn back – but his head is turned so that it is at a slightly less acute angle facing the other way to his body. The book is the device justifying these contortions. The Christ Child *may* have been attending to his little bird (symbolic meanings have been suggested for these birds which were often represented with the Christ Child, yet the cruel truth of the matter is that live birds were given to little children as toys), but he has now turned to focus his gaze upwards at his mother's book of prayers or of pious devotions, such as literate women were expected to own. Contact between the mother and child consists of this shared attention, and of her hand supporting his foot – creating a semi-circular pattern in the lower part of the picture. We may think of the panel being subdivided into thirds along its width as well as its length: the Virgin's face in the middle third, and most of the Christ Child also. (Notice that his little toe marks off a third of the width of the panel at the lower edge of the picture.) The 'centring' helps to focus our attention, and is also an iconic device – the 'centre-stage' is the most 'important' space on the picture plane. But his face is exactly *half*-turned to the book – his nose marks the first third of the panel's width. (You should check all this with a ruler if you haven't noticed it before.) Since, in defiance of historical truth, we must assume the Virgin to be reading a book of Christian devotion, the

child's serious contemplation may be taken as prospective: he is shown as *looking forward* to the truths asserted in the book, that is, the crucifixion and the redemption of humankind. The fact that he must look heavenwards to see the book, in an attitude associated with pious martyr saints submitting to divine will, is not without its resonance.

Finally, a word about the physical types of the *Solly Madonna*. The schematically round faces, with the features all inscribed within a wide-based triangle pointing downwards, are derived from a formula associated with Perugino. We are mainly struck by how artificial and saccharine-sweet the formula looks, but Perugino's contemporaries found the rose-bud mouths, straight short noses and wide-spaced eyes appealing and beautiful. The fingers of the Virgin's right hand are disposed in a gesture of studied refinement. The Christ Child is almost a parody of plump babyhood: his bottom half looks positively inflated. If we measure his body length in relation to the length of his head, we find that it is about three-and-a-half heads long – proportions which account for his pin-headed look.

The poses of the figures in the *Tempi Madonna* are both more complex, although the overall effect seems clear and simple. The Virgin stands at an angle to the picture plane, left shoulder drawn back, face almost in pure profile. The Child's body is pressed against hers on the same axis – but in mirror image; thus it is his right shoulder which is drawn back. He turns his head towards the front of the picture, so that we see Mary and the Child cheek to cheek, her head slightly inclined towards him, his head slightly raised to her.

The twisting and turning of both figures not only adds interest and grace to the picture – the Virgin is not as four-square as in the *Solly Madonna* – but it also means that a single clear outline, a single shape, can be formed by both figures, not, as in the earlier painting, by Mary entirely 'containing' the infant. (Now compare Colour plate 6 with Donatello's *Pazzi Madonna*, Plate 14.) The bodies also define their own three-dimensional space, whereas in the *Solly Madonna* the accessory of the book was required to do this. The embrace of Mother and Child in the *Tempi Madonna* is mutual, but subtly differentiated. Mary focuses entirely on the child; he, on the other hand, gazes rather pensively out of the picture – not directly at us, but unfocused into the distance. A viewer sensitive to the Christian implications of the scene will once again be tempted to read this meditative and serious gaze as prospective, a foreknowledge of the Passion to come. But in this painting Raphael is content with this most delicate of hints, which we are free to ignore if we wish merely to delight in the idealized domestic aspect of the theme.

The facial types of mother and child are no longer as formulaic as in the *Solly Madonna*, or rather the formula has changed: mouths are widened, there is a greater use of shadows for modelling, hair is no longer drawn stroke by silky brush stroke. The Virgin's grasp of the child is firm, not as insistently ladylike as the gesture of her right hand in Colour Plate 5. There is a far greater use of shadow modelling on the figures in general; most strikingly, on the baby's plump flesh. He is no longer as schematic, to the point of deformation, as in the *Solly Madonna*. And his bodily proportions have been reduced to three heads.

The greatest change however comes in the latest of the entire series, the *Large Cowper Madonna* (Colour plate 7). As in the *Tempi Madonna*, the figures are turned from the picture plane and represented as virtually mirror images (note the extension of the Virgin's right arm, the child's left arm) with the striking exception of their faces, hers in nearly pure profile, his in full face. But the three-dimensional space defined by these poses is far deeper than that in the *Tempi Madonna*. We can see this in the way the Virgin's knees are spread to hold the cushion on which the child is seated (the pose is clarified through the way in which his naked round legs are also spread). The standing Virgin in the *Tempi Madonna* could not, of course, be shown straddling space in this way. Mary's left knee, facing us, seems to protrude out of the picture – and her right hand is actually cut off by the frame of the panel. These details contribute to our sense of the figures being closer to us than those in Colour Plates 5 and 6. But the most striking evidence of the artist's intention to break out of the self-containment of the earlier Madonna pictures is the child's direct address to the viewer. Mary is absorbed by him, but he, although clinging to his mother with the playful and unconsciously possessive gesture of a real child, laughingly engages our gaze. The centre of our attention has been subtly shifted, from the Virgin mother of Christ, to Christ Incarnate. Notice how the Virgin's left hand on her breast delicately suggests a gesture of reverence.

The spread-kneed and twisting poses – more strained and artificial than they look – are indebted in the first instance to Leonardo who evolved them, and in the second to Michelangelo who was to take them further (compare Colour plate 7 with Plate 15, Michelangelo's *Taddei Tondo*). Michelangelo is also the influence behind the majestic bulk of the figures, as Leonardo is behind the increased use of shadow and the facial types. But the composition as a whole, its grave sweetness, the complexity of the abstract harmonies of shapes and lines (notice the parallels described by the Virgin's left arm and the child's left leg, and the way the trapezoid outline of the figures is echoed in the inner shape above the Virgin's left thigh), above all the equilibrium between formula and realism – all these are entirely Raphael's own achievements. They reveal themselves to us only with prolonged looking, and through looking at many examples of the genre. In the same way, the finished harmonies were revealed to Raphael himself through many drawings, from rough sketches of Madonna and Child schemata (formulaic outlines), through notes from life, through contemplation of other artists' work, through many stages of variations on the theme.

Because we are dealing only with imperfect colour reproductions, it is not appropriate to lay too much stress on the use of colour and brush stroke in these paintings. You should however note the way a very few hues – mainly red, blue, yellow and white – have been manipulated and balanced, broad effects against delicate traceries, opaque against translucent. Think also of the permutations of skin/cloth, smooth/dimpled, etc. All of these have their psychological impact on the viewer, and each painting on the theme explores a subtly different emotional range.

It is to be hoped that this detailed pictorial analysis has demonstrated that the classification of works of art into genres or kinds of subject-matter is significant in that each genre, or sub-genre, permitted innovation *within* a relatively restricted range of choices, conventions and expectations. The practice of collecting which became more widespread in the sixteenth century encouraged experimentation within a relatively autonomous, specialized 'game' in which the rules were well known to the initiated. In this particular example (genre: religious art; sub-genre: Madonna and Child image), certain expectations had to be met: frivolous or hostile poses or expressions would, for example, have been unacceptable. Within those limitations, however, the artist has experimented with both content (different costumes; accessories such as the bird, the book, the cushion) and form, thus reinforcing and extending simultaneously the rules and possibilities of this particular 'game'.

6 THE RISE OF THE ACADEMIES

The growth of collecting, as we have seen, consolidated and brought into greater prominence the classification of art into different genres. This was also the effect of the rise of the academies.

By the end of the eighteenth century the training of professional artists in Western Europe had undergone a profound change. Instead of being apprenticed, like any craftsman, to a master licensed to practise his trade by a guild, most painters and many sculptors were now receiving their early training in art schools – the academies to which Gombrich refers throughout Chapter V of *Art and Illusion* (which we'll be looking at later).

The early academies were formed in Italy in the sixteenth century, both as discussion groups led by painters and connoisseurs, and to provide artists with additional practice in drawing, especially in copying antique sculpture. The rise of the academies was part of a general attempt by artists to modify their social status, to differentiate themselves from other craftsmen. By claiming for painting the standing of a 'Liberal Art' founded in theory, they could identify themselves with the learned professions.

The first formal art academy, which was a teaching body as well as a kind of honorary society, was founded in Florence in 1562 by the artist-courtier Giorgio Vasari under the aegis of the Grand Duke Cosimo I. Needless to say, the latter's primary concern was not to benefit the artists. As the founder of what was in effect a brand-new monarchy, a despotic ruler over a city and region traditionally devoted to the forms of republican government, he wished to harness art to legitimize and publicize his own standing and his dynastic aspirations. To this end he set about controlling not only the production of art but also the training of artists.

Most of the drawing books illustrated by Gombrich in Chapter V of *Art and Illusion* exemplify the ideas and methods of Italian academies for the benefit of northern European artists. They were compiled by northern artists who had either made the trip across the Alps to Venice and Rome, or had studied Italian art at second hand. But in one country the political lessons of the Grand Duke's patronage were heeded especially well. In the mid-seventeenth century the ministers of the French crown, busy consolidating the absolute rule of monarchy, helped found and then fostered the French Royal Academy of Painting and Sculpture. From 1664 it not only became responsible for the education of many French artists, but also monopolized the privilege of public art exhibitions. (That is, no one could legally organize an art exhibition open to the public except the Royal Academy.) In 1666 the French Academy in Rome was established as a post-graduate school in which prize-winning students could absorb the grand Italian manner, studying especially the works of the masters of the High Renaissance, Michelangelo and Raphael.

Like the French state itself, the Academy was a highly centralized, bureaucratic and hierarchic institution. Taking over ideas about art which had become current in Renaissance Italy, it codified them far more rigidly and prescriptively than the Italians had done. Since later academies through Europe, including the British Royal Academy finally established in 1768, were profoundly influenced by the French Academy, the theories propounded in the latter came to permeate thinking about art (if not always the practice of art) all over Europe. We are still to a great extent conditioned by these ideas, even if only in rejecting them.

There was in the seventeenth and eighteenth centuries an important debate about the relative importance of *colour* and *linear design*. Although this was never totally resolved in favour of the latter, design (from the Italian *disegno*) was at the basis of academic training. The word, however, had different connotations from those we associate with it. It meant, in the first instance, *drawing*, in the sense in which it is illustrated in the drawing books cited by Gombrich. But, equally if not even more importantly, it also meant arriving at a composition of the work as a whole. That idea, in turn, involved far more than our sense of constructing a 'pleasing arrangement'. To design a work of art meant to invest it with meaning: a successful composition had to express the sense of a pictured scene; it had to reveal this sense to the viewer; it had to persuade or stimulate the viewer's intellect and emotions to some desired end. In academic art theory, the composition of a work of visual art was thought of as not unlike that of a literary work. The various elements of the image, like the vocabulary of a piece of literature, had to be suited to the sense and purpose of the work as a whole: an elevated image must not admit coarse or vulgar effects, a lyrical image should be poetical in every detail, and so on. All the elements had to work together, and a proper balance found between copiousness and variety on the one hand and clarity and unity on the other. Finally, design in this academic sense also implied choosing, or inventing, the most telling moment or aspect of a scene, the viewpoint from which it must appear to the viewer – not only in the optical sense but also intellectually and imaginatively.

7 THE HIERARCHY OF THE GENRES: 'HISTORY PAINTING'

During the Italian Renaissance attempts were made to place the increasing number of genres or kinds of subject-matter of art into rank order, by analogy with ancient Graeco-Roman theories of literary genres. This hierarchic system was applied mainly to painting, although it has also been applied to sculpture. The hierarchy of genres was codified by Félibien, in the preface to the 1669 publication of lectures he had delivered at the French Academy in 1667. This hierarchy continued to be influential in European academies well into the nineteenth century, but, as a system of *evaluation*, influences us little today. We may continue to *classify* works of art according to genre, but such a classification has little connection with the value we attach to them. History painting was put at the top of the hierarchy.

A *history painting* is a type of painting representing the human figure, which illustrates religious, historic or legendary narrative incidents or allegories of a grand, didactic, high-minded and noble kind.

It is not to be wondered at that the French Academy put *narrative* paintings of this kind at the top of the hierarchy. For narrative painting or sculpture required, it was felt, the greatest intellectual and imaginative effort to design or compose, in the sense in which design has been outlined above. The narrative art they had in mind was of the kind named in Italian *istoria* (history), in French *histoire*, and in English *history* (the latter two of which could mean both history and story), from the Latin *historia*, 'story' or 'narrative'. As we have seen, much medieval art was concerned with religious subject-matter. When the academies attributed status to each of the genres, religious narrative (episodes from the lives of the saints, Christ and the Virgin) was seen as one of the most important and most elevated *kinds* or sub-categories of history painting and the term 'history' was often applied retrospectively to earlier religious narratives. (Studies of individual saints or of Christ, 'religious portraits', were also included within the history genre, even where the narrative element was slight or non-existent.)

As the visual arts expanded their repertory during the Renaissance, to include secular as well as religious subjects, and especially to glorify secular patrons, both patrons and artists naturally turned to themes from classical mythology, literature and history, all regarded as valid and important sub-genres within the broad genre or category, 'history painting'. Until recently, these had formed the basis of European high culture, and were studied by all educated persons. In Renaissance Italy, mythological scenes were called *favole* (fables) or *poesie* (poems) to distinguish them from other narratives. And although many such scenes were primarily poetic or even erotic in their appeal, their status became more or less equivalent to more high-minded *istoria* in the academic hierarchy. Calls for 'purging' art of these subjects recurred, however, at various times in the eighteenth and early nineteenth centuries. Those of you who go on to study A206, *The Enlightenment*, will learn how the French eighteenth-century artist, Boucher, was criticized for polluting the history genre with (allegedly) gratuitously erotic scenes from ancient mythology. Even if displayed in a semi-private context, like a reception room in a private palace, history painting was meant to exemplify public virtues, or to assert some other public statement such as the high moral and social status of the owner.

History painting and its sculptural analogues were held, in academic thought, to be the visual equivalent of the literary genres rated highest in classical – that is, ancient Graeco-Roman – literary theory: epic and tragedy, relating the deeds of people *greater than ourselves*. Leon Battista Alberti, the fifteenth-century author of a famous treatise, *On Painting*, had already drawn this comparison, adding that *istoria* was therefore suited to the decoration of public buildings and the palaces of the great. The prestige of history painting was in this way related both to the moral and social stature of its subjects and to the high status of its patrons.

Italian Renaissance artists – none more than Michelangelo – had found the visual components of a grand manner (the equivalent of the elevated, epic style in poetry) in classical art, and employed them even for works in the service of Christianity. A famous example is Michelangelo's *Last Judgment* in the Sistine Chapel in the Vatican (Plate 16). It aroused controversy shortly after it was completed because Michelangelo had painted all his figures 'classically' nude, and this came to be felt as inappropriate over the altar in the papal chapel. After Michelangelo's death a young artist he had befriended was hired to cover up some of the most glaring nude passages, and his draperies and veils are still visible today.

By the eighteenth century history painting and sculpture were identified with a classical style as much as with classical content. It also became more common for the genre to include subjects from more recent literary texts and historical events. Even when the *deeds of the great* to be depicted were not drawn from Graeco-Roman antiquity, but from national history, from vernacular (that is, not Greek or Latin) literature, or from contemporary events, couching them in the visual language of classical art as reinterpreted by the Renaissance masters was the accepted method of *idealization*: investing the image with *universal significance*. Thus as late as 1777–83, James Barry, one of the few exponents of the grand manner in Britain, painted mural-sized canvases of *The Progress of Human Culture Guided by the Arts* for the Great Room of the Royal Society of Arts in London in a rather fevered Michelangelesque idiom (Plate 17). The painting comments on the artist's claim to be able to offer something useful to society.

Although history painting continued to be associated with the large mural scale (with life-size or over life-size figures) on which it had been conceived in the Renaissance, the rise of collecting saw its translation also to the moderate scale of the portable easel painting. One man can be said to have been responsible for this development: the French-born painter Nicolas Poussin (1594–1665), resident for most of his working life in Rome. Enormously serious and ambitious, he was virtually self-taught, at least in comparison with the Italian artists with whom he competed after his arrival in Rome in 1624. Having established a certain reputation with easel paintings of battle scenes and poetical fantasies on mythological themes – all collectors' pieces, sub-genres later recognized but uncodified by the Royal Academies – he failed in critical esteem with his first Italian essays on the monumental scale, two altar-pieces for Roman churches. Eighteen unhappy months in Paris in the service of the French king (1640–2) convinced him finally of his lack of aptitude for large-scale decoration, but acquainted him with a group of professional men, collectors and connoisseurs as serious and high-minded as he. For the rest of his life he served this clientèle on a mail-order basis, supplying them with series and single canvases of biblical and other sacred scenes, as well as subjects from ancient history. These were painted in a passionately austere classicizing style derived from ancient sculpture, the reconstruction of ancient architecture, and High Renaissance works, principally those of Raphael (see, for example, Plate 18).

Poussin's portable *istorie*, available for study in Paris and executed by a native French artist, not unnaturally became touchstones for the French Royal Academy and, through its influence, for English and other northern European academicians. In Italy, the predilection for the life-scale *istoria* led seventeenth-century artists to evolve portable multi-figure narrative compositions in half-length (compare this development of easel painting with previous remarks on the half-length Madonna formula, pp.58–9). But many northern academic artists followed Poussin's example, painting full-length history pictures on a moderate scale for academy exhibitions, for collectors, and, in the all-too-frequent absence of commissions, as a basis for popular reproductions through engraving (another means of ensuring the public status of a work) which would be sold to recoup the costs of the paintings themselves.

It is probably this last procedure which led to the development of the modern-dress history painting. Significantly, the turning point came with a picture by an American, Benjamin West (1738–1820), who was untrained in drawing from the antique and in other academic formulae. He may even have misunderstood the correct, generalized meaning of the term *history painting*. Having set himself up in London after a study trip to Italy, West (who was later to become the second president of the Royal Academy) realized the potential to artists of the new feeling of national pride which had grown up in the general public, who were able to buy an engraving or attend an exhibition, but were not themselves connoisseurs of art or attuned to the values of the academies. *The Death of General Wolfe* (Colour plate 8), West's most popular work, exhibited at the Academy in 1771, was reputed to have earned him as much as £15,000 from sales of the engraving (a far greater sum in the 1770s than it would be in today's currency). It commemorated, about a decade after the event, the death of General James Wolfe, the British commander, at the very moment of victory over the French at Quebec – a victory which secured Britain's hold over Canada.

Upon hearing of the painter's plan to depict the scene in contemporary dress, rather than in classical drapes, King George III is reported to have said, 'very ridiculous to exhibit heroes in coats, breeches and cock'd hats'. Here we have an example of the way in which painters working in a particular genre, thereby arousing a certain set of expectations as to the style or method of depiction they should employ, can create shock when they do not meet those expectations. In this case, the interpretation put upon the painting was influenced by the traditions and expectations associated with its kind of subject-matter (or genre). Yet despite all the realistic details, including the body paint on the Red Indian brave, West's picture is not at all factual. Only three men are thought to have witnessed Wolfe's death – none of them Indian. West has cleverly employed conventions of the grand manner while rejecting the particular academic formula of classical drapery (although the symbolic figure of the Indian enables him to sneak in a classical nude). The main group of the dying general supported by his officers is based on the traditional schema (conventional plan or outline) of a *Lamentation*, the mourning over the body of Christ before his burial. West must have seen countless representations of this scene on his Italian tour. Wolfe's raised eyes and foreshortened face recall the imagery used to depict ecstatic saints and martyrs – imagery itself derived from an ancient prototype, the sculptural group of Laocoon and his sons being crushed to death by giant serpents, discovered in 1506 and now in the Vatican museum (Plate 19).

By composing his modern-dress history with reference to such 'universal' formulae, the artist imparted to the death of a British national hero the absolute significance of a religious icon. This example also demonstrates the extent to which the genre of history painting is not the representation of a model actually available to the artist (like a scene to be photographed), but the result of invention. Academic study, both of drawing from life and of formulae from earlier art, is intended to facilitate invention, to furnish the bricks, as it were, from which an imaginary structure may be built up. Realism, or a faithful imitation of the visible world, is not a priority for the history painter preoccupied with depicting people *greater than ourselves* in scenes uncommon in reality. We encounter again the idea that the different genres generate their own conventions, expectations and treatment of formal elements.

West's innovation had immediate successors, and the painting of serious moralizing narrative scenes, whether from modern life or on literary themes, in historically appropriate dress became an acceptable mode, widely popular especially in England and France. As a sub-genre it became nearly conflated with another of the academies' codified types, the painting of everyday subjects, to which we shall turn presently.

Those aspects of *istoria* associated with it in the Renaissance and in academic theory of the seventeenth and eighteenth centuries continued, however, to signify, and still signify today, 'high art'. First amongst these is *scale*, and its implication of *public* function. You should recall here Oldenburg's imaginary monuments and his 'gigantic' clothes-peg (Plate 13). While the female nude is more often an erotic motif than a heroic one, the muscular male nude almost always implies heroism. In this light the TUC monument of *The Spirit of Trade Unionism* (p.47) is an example of 'history' sculpture. Classicism, the return to Graeco-Roman formulae, also invests works of art with 'elevated' meaning. All of these still signal to us high status, a reference to the deeds of those 'greater than ourselves'. The academic values remain potent, even if only to be challenged.

8 PORTRAITURE

Next in the hierarchy of the genres as codified in the French Royal Academy and in academies through Europe was *portraiture*, specifically life-size or larger than life-size portraiture of the great and powerful. To *portray* means to make a likeness of, or to describe graphically. We have already discussed the differences between public portraiture status and more intimate forms, usually on a smaller scale, so we won't expand on it here, other than to point out a few particulars of academic theory and practice.

By the seventeenth century portraiture was the most widely commissioned form of imagery throughout Europe among the middle classes as well as the aristocracy. At this time conventions of portraiture were established, through which patrons and artists could rapidly come to an understanding. Format related to social status, function and cost. A full-length life-size portrait implied higher status, a more public function, and cost more than a mere 'head'. A new, medium-priced format was devised: an elongated bust-length, large enough to include the arms and hands. Church dignitaries were usually shown seated, a convention imitating Raphael's famous portraits of Popes Julius II (Plate 20) and Leo X. Even portrait backgrounds were formalized: a great loop of drapery, a column, glimpses of landscape through an open window or above a balustrade were customary appurtenances of the aristocratic portrait from the seventeenth to the eighteenth centuries and do not imply that the sitter actually posed in such a setting. By the eighteenth century, the successful portraitist might well concentrate only on the sitter's face, while anonymous specialists provided conventional draperies, landscapes, even hands, on an assembly-line basis for more than one painter's studio.

But the most significant portrait conventions were probably those suggested by the hierarchic rating of pictorial genres. These conventions, promoted by the academies, furnished artists with the means of 'elevating' the dignity of their sitters through the use of pictorial conventions normally associated with the history genre. Just as certain iconic conventions such as those of kingship or of various types of religious imagery, could be adapted to give additional resonance to a portrait, so the borrowing of formulae associated with the highest genre, history painting, could confer upon sitters the nobility of epic or tragic heroes. Sitters could be depicted in the guise of a figure from literature, history, mythology or the Bible. In practice this usually came to mean the adaptation of classical formulae such as the heroic male nude (see for example illustrations 123, 125 and 126 in *Art and Illusion*) or antique drapery and armour, even for contemporary subjects. Thus Sir Joshua Reynolds, a portraitist much patronized by the aristocracy and the first president of the British Royal Academy, in the lectures he delivered to students between 1769 and 1790, advocated:

> He therefore who in his practice of portrait-painting wishes to dignify his subject, which we will suppose to be a lady, will not paint her in the modern dress, the familiarity of which alone is sufficient to destroy all dignity. He takes care that his work shall correspond to those ideas and that imagination which he knows will regulate the judgment of others; and therefore dresses his figure something with the general air of the antique for the sake of dignity, and preserves something of the modern for the sake of likeness. (Sir Joshua Reynolds, *Discourse VII*, 1776)

You will find an example of this procedure in Reynolds' portrait of Lady Elizabeth Delmé and her children (illustration 19 in *Art and Illusion*). 'For the sake of likeness', Lady Elizabeth's hair is dressed more or less in current fashion; her bodice, however, is an eighteenth-century approximation to ancient costume, and the great cloak draped about her legs is a 'grand manner' exaggeration of antique drapery. (Compare this with the frontispiece of *Art and Illusion*, and the real thing shown in Gombrich's illustration 97.) The Delmé children, needing no dignifying, are pictured in the real dress of the period. But just to make things more complicated, even this is not purely 'modern' but makes a reference to past art. The little boy wears a 'Van Dyck' velvet suit, a fashion which continued to be popular for upper-class little English boys through the early years of our own century. It is an imitation of the dress worn in the seventeenth-century portraits of King Charles I and of his children by the Flemish-born court painter Van Dyck. As Reynolds said in the same lecture, 'The great variety of excellent portraits with which Vandyck has enriched this nation, we are not content to admire for their real excellence, but extend our approbation even to the dress which happened to be the fashion of that age'.

Reynolds, however, had also employed more drastic means of 'elevating' portraiture to the higher status of history painting. For some fifteen years before the completion of *Lady Elizabeth Delmé and her Children*, he had specialized in posing his sitters in classicizing *tableaux vivants* – suitable charades truly conflating (combining) portraiture with narrative, and borrowing figure poses and other motifs from a variety of ancient and Italianate works of art. Through showing his works in this mode at the Royal Academy exhibitions, he had succeeded in educating both patrons and younger artists. Perhaps the most famous example, and the best documented, is his painting of the three beautiful Montgomery sisters, reproduced in Plate 22, *Three Ladies Adorning a Term of Hymen*. (A 'term' is a pillar or pilaster which at its top is transformed into a human half-figure or bust, or the half-figure of an animal. Hymen was the Greek god of marriage. You may sometime wish to read Professor Gombrich's illuminating article on this painting, 'Reynolds's theory and practice of imitation', *Norm and Form*.)

Reynolds' justification of artistic borrowing is not only a supreme statement of academic doctrine, but also an insider's view of artistic autonomy. In his twelfth discourse, delivered at the annual prize-giving ceremony of the Royal Academy, 10 December, 1784, he speaks of artists borrowing, not from 'mere poverty' but in order 'to possess peculiar rarities' while enriching 'the general store' of art:

> [...] such men surely need not be ashamed of that friendly intercourse which ought to exist among Artists, of receiving from the dead and giving to the living, and perhaps to those who are yet unborn.
>
> The daily food and nourishment of the mind of an Artist is found in the great works of his predecessors.

It could be argued, however, that the more informal, natural portraits of Ramsay, the eighteenth-century Scottish painter, and of French artists made a greater impact on portraiture of the future. They produced images based on imagination, sympathy and perception rather than on formulaic or anachronistic representations of power and status.

While full-length portraiture on the scale of life remained, as already said, the most prestigious for the patron and the most lucrative for the artist, a more informal type of portraiture evolved in association with the next lower pictorial genre in the academic hierarchy, which has come to be called, confusingly, by its nineteenth-century appellation of *genre*. (You need to look out for the context as well as the presence or absence of the article to know whether an author is speaking of 'a genre', meaning 'one of the genres', or of '*genre*', the category to be discussed in the next section.) Plate 21 is an early example of this kind of portrait, by the Dutch painter Thomas de Keyser (1596 or 1597–1667). Perhaps the most important feature of this kind of picture is its size; please assess this carefully with the aid of a measuring tape, and try to imagine the effect the painting would have on this scale.

9 'GENRE'

Although the word, *genre*, used to describe *one* of the genres, is relatively new (it gained common currency in the nineteenth century), the pictorial category which it encompasses is very old, and complex. It is best translated (if cautiously) as the *depiction of everyday life*. In the same way that history painting was equated with the literary genres of epic and tragedy – in ancient literary theory the depiction of the deeds of 'people greater than ourselves' – so the portrayal of everyday life was related to comedy, a less elevated (if not *necessarily* humorous) genre, the representation of 'the habits of private citizens', of people 'like ourselves, or worse than ourselves'. Most genre paintings have a narrative function: they depict stories, incidents and deeds, or, at the very least, a typical 'activity'.

Pliny the Elder (23–79 AD), a Roman writer and early source for the history of ancient art, singles out specialists in the painting of country pursuits, of 'barbers' shops and cobblers' stalls'. In his *Ten Books on Architecture* (*c.*1450) Leon Battista Alberti writes of the pleasure we derive from 'paintings depicting [...] fishing, hunting, swimming, the games of shepherds'. Whereas *istoria* 'should be used for public buildings and the dwellings of the great' the representation of the 'life of the peasants' is most suitable for country villas, 'for it is the most pleasing of all'.

By no means always cheap, but invariably cheerful, the depiction of everyday life, both in painting and sculpture, survived the serious-minded ideals of art both of the Middle Ages and of the academies. One might say, very broadly, that its survival was ensured through the following tactics: *marginalization* and *symbolism*.

While the great themes of Christian art were unfolded in the main pictorial and sculptural fields – whether on altars and in aisles, on the walls of chapels and the main portals of churches, in stained glass, in illuminated manuscripts of devotional books – *genre* scenes found a place in odd corners: literally in the margins of manuscripts, on sculpted capitals, on misericords – the little wooden supports carved on the underside of choir stalls to ease the rigours of standing during services. With the rise of secular patronage, the activities of guild members might be illustrated on the edges of the stained glass windows they had donated. Scenes of the life of peasants showing the labours of the months moved centre stage in the illuminated Books of Hours, the devotional books for laymen and women arranged according to the calendar. And, of course, *genre* subjects were favoured in much secular domestic decoration: on painted panelling (see *Art and Illusion*, illustration 107), on tapestries and painted clothes, bed-hangings, kitchen implements, etc. The scenes detailed by Alberti found a place even in fresco decoration, especially in the country retreats of townspeople. As the collecting of portable paintings evolved, *genre* came to be an acceptable subject of easel paintings alongside the other 'lesser' genres (landscape and still life). From the late fifteenth century it often became overtly comical in tone: the visible activities of 'people worse than ourselves', that is, rustics, labourers, market-stall keepers – since 'ourselves' was understood to mean the picture-owning classes. In northern Europe the hated tax collectors were subjects of pictorial satire, together with such comical themes, drawn from proverbs and popular theatre, as 'the ill-matched lovers' (youth and age), 'concupiscent love' (prostitutes, procuresses and their clients), fortune tellers, quack doctors and dentists, card sharps, and their gullible victims. Jan Molenaer's *The Dentist* is an example of a seventeenth-century *genre* painting (Plate 23). It shows a country bumpkin having his tooth extracted. Notice the pickpocket stealing a duck from the watching woman's basket. In seventeenth-century Holland *genre* painting became the dominant activity of artists such as Ostade, Steen, Metsu, Ter Borch, Vermeer and de Hooch, who each specialized in sub-categories such as peasant and tavern scenes or musical or genteel drinking parties.

Like proverbs, these subjects were meant to point a moral, to symbolize some meaning not necessarily visible to the untutored eye. At a time when the whole world of nature and of culture was seen *sub specie aeternitatis*, that is, from the point of view of eternity, moralizing came naturally. Human life was brief, and our conduct in this life entailed consequences, blissful or terrible, for all eternity. God was active throughout creation, and reality a kind of rebus, a riddle or parable in which higher meanings were disguised, but visible to those who learned to see.

Like plays performed in the theatre, painted scenes of everyday life could testify to human folly and symbolize, for example, such concepts as the seven capital sins, those from which all other sins follow: pride, envy, avarice, *luxuria* or lust, gluttony, anger, sloth. Colour Plate 9 reproduces the so-called *Tabletop of the Seven Deadly Sins and the Four Last Things*, painted by the Dutch artist Hieronymus Bosch (*c.*1450–1516). This panel, probably intended as an aid to meditation, is a very model of symbolic or moralizing *genre*. It is exceptional in being both very early and very explicit. The condition of humankind is presented in a series of small images disposed in a circle around the ever-watchful eye of God, in whose pupil Christ emerges from the tomb, displaying the wounds acquired on humanity's behalf. Below him is inscribed 'Beware, beware, God sees'. We hardly need the Latin captions to grasp which sin is exemplified in each little scene of everyday life. Not only the lower orders, but all conditions of society are castigated here: the well-fed scholar dozing before the fire neglects his spiritual duties, symbolized by the woman holding out a rosary; aristocratic lovers inside a tent demonstrate the follies of lust; a young housewife admiring her new coif, unaware that her mirror is held by a demon, has fallen prey to vanity, or pride; avarice is shown by a judge accepting bribes. Perhaps you can pick out the other sins yourself. In the four corners of the panel are shown the 'Last Four Things': death, the Last Judgment, Heaven, and Hell in which each earthly sin is appropriately punished. The captions above and below the central image reinforce the moral: if only humankind were wise, and considered the consequence of earthly acts!

Throughout Europe, pictorial and sculptural *genre* survived because it was a way of having one's cake and eating it too. The satisfaction of asserting moral or social superiority was joined to the enjoyment of a faithful imitation of observable reality, such as you may have derived from the details of Colour Plate 9. Many of the Victorian paintings of everyday life which you will meet later in the course combine precisely the same appeal: the artist seems to hold up a mirror to life as his viewers might have known it, but the reflection is skewed to point a moral or reveal some other meaning not immediately visible to the eye and which requires verbal translation.

Although the people represented in *genre* are not necessarily the same people who are likely to view or collect *genre* pictures, the appeal of this type of image is wider than that of history painting. Where history painting presumes that the viewer knows something of the repertory of grand-manner art, can recognize literary allusions, and appreciates an approach to formal elements which derives little from any first-hand observation of the real world, *genre* relies on the viewer's acquiescence to a dominant ideology (as in the matter of social hierarchy or sexual morality, for example) and familiarity with popular culture (such as proverbs, puns, commonplace tags). But above all, *genre* pleases because we all like to recognize ourselves or our neighbours, our circumstances and physical surroundings. Even the unlearned viewer appreciates a faithful imitation of real life.

The development of oil painting on small-scale panel or canvas made possible a particularly high imitative fidelity: the 'code' of oil painting enables a very wide range of colour and lustre effects, and the suggestion of the surface texture of many different kinds of materials and of the passage of light through different kinds of space and media, such as glass or water. Although it is now established that the fifteenth-century Netherlandish painter Jan Van Eyck (d.1441) did not 'invent' painting in oils, as was once thought, it is certainly true that he brought the technique to a state of mimetic mastery which has never been surpassed (see illustrations 171 and 180 in *Art and Illusion*). (A mimetic work – from the Greek, *mimesis*, 'imitation' – is one which attempts a close degree of imitation, or resemblance, to the object(s) it represents.) Van Eyck's influence on northern European painting resulted in even the Italians conceding the superiority of the northerners in this branch of art. By the sixteenth century artists and connoisseurs thought of European art as being divided into two major branches: the Italianate, with its command of the large scale, of 'design', and its appropriation of the visual and literary repertory of Graeco-Roman antiquity; and the northern European, mainly Netherlandish or German, expert in small-scale mimesis. (Of course, this broad division does not begin to do justice either to local variants or to individual artists; you should also remember that both the Italians and the northerners attempted to complement their own special skills by learning from each other.)

The recognition of these areas of specialism led Italian collectors to seek out northern artists, or their products, to supply examples of the 'lesser' genres, including *genre*; later, the academically minded too were able to delight in this kind of art, as long as 'it knew its place'. Conflict ensued mainly when the exponents of 'lesser genres' attempted to treat elevated subjects in the less grand, mimetic mode associated with the 'lower'. The 'shock value' of such paintings arises when the treatment of a subject does not conform with conventional expectations.

A famous case in point is a painting of Saint Matthew executed by a northern Italian artist, Michelangelo Merisi (1573–1610) better known as Caravaggio after the Lombard town where he was born (Plate 24). Migrating from his native region to Rome as a very young man, he acquired a reputation among wealthy collectors for highly mimetic still-lifes and paintings of half-length figures of slightly disreputable youths: musicians, cardsharpers, fortune-tellers, seductive fruit-sellers, Roman street boys, all executed with the minute attention to surface detail characteristic of Netherlandish and German painting, which was very influential in Lombardy. That such works included homo-erotic elements can in part be accounted for by Caravaggio's homosexuality. Sometime in the late 1590s he was commissioned, probably through the intervention of one of his collector patrons who was a Cardinal, to complete the pictorial decoration of a chapel dedicated to Saint Matthew in the Roman church of San Luigi dei Francesi. The painting reproduced in Plate 24 was originally intended for the altarpiece. However, as the seventeenth-century chronicler Bellori records,

> [...] the priests removed the *Saint Matthew*, [Caravaggio's] first public work, from the altar, saying that the figure had no decorum, did not look like a saint, sitting with crossed legs and with his feet crudely exposed to the people. Marchese Vincenzo Giustiniani [a famous collector] intervened on behalf of Caravaggio, arranging with the priests to take the painting for himself and to have a second one made which is now there. Giustiniani took Caravaggio's first *Saint Matthew* into his house, placing it together with three other Evangelists by the most celebrated painters of the time, Guido, Domenichino and Albani. (Cited in W. Friedlander, *Caravaggio Studies*, p.178)

Caravaggio was in fact following Lombard examples – albeit none of them an altarpiece – of depicting Saint Matthew as a proletarian; the saint's attribute, a winged angel, is shown having to guide his hand to form the letters of his gospel. But this return to 'early Christian simplicity' was too radical. That the author of the first gospel, the publican or tax collector summoned by Jesus to follow him, should be represented as illiterate was bad enough; that he should cross his legs and show his dirty feet above the altar table, like a rough labourer at an inn, was obviously too much. But note that Caravaggio's *genre*-like treatment, unacceptable in an altarpiece, found favour in the secular context of an art collection, where its naturalism did not shock, and the piquant contrast between the bewildered elderly workingman and the smart young angel could be savoured. Note also the close relationship here between beholders' expectations and the meanings derived from – or denied in – such a painting.

Centuries after *genre* painting had seemingly ousted *istoria* from the affections of collectors, the conventions codified in the academic hierarchy of the genres still had power to convey meaning. Plate 25 reproduces *The Stonebreakers*, a painting nearly two metres tall and three metres long, executed in 1849 and exhibited at the Salon – the officially sponsored annual public exhibition in Paris – of 1850–1 by the French artist Courbet. As he wrote to a friend, Courbet had encountered the two labourers along the road – 'it is rare to meet the most complete expression of poverty' – and had invited them to pose for him in his studio. The picture employs the scale of history painting, but none of its devices of composition, or classical or literary allusions, etc., to 'heroize' the two men. They do not invite our empathy or sympathy, since they turn their backs to us and their faces are hidden from us; the landscape rising behind them seems to force them even closer to the stones at which they labour, and they themselves, as contemporary critics observed, are painted to seem no more important than the carefully depicted stones.

Courbet continues his letter describing the picture by stating his artistic programme: the necessity for taking art 'into the lower depth' ('*encanailler l'art*') since for too long artists have relied on 'an idea and a cartoon'. This is a direct reference to the academic practice of idealizing and meticulous design. A cartoon, in this context, is a full-scale drawing, the result of many preparatory drawings, used to transfer the outlines of the main feature of a composition onto panel, canvas or wall. Courbet implies that his painting relies only on direct observation of his models, 'encoded' into paint with the minimum of intellectual transformation or invention, unlike conventional academic history painting.

The Stonebreakers was exhibited at the very moment when the French bourgeoisie, under Louis-Napoleon, had re-established itself in power after the proletarian uprisings of 1848. Simply by treating his subject on the monumental scale of history painting, devoid of the charm of overt symbolism of traditional small-scale *genre*, Courbet seemed to be allying himself with the defeated revolutionaries, to be making a left-wing political statement. Worse: by avoiding all other aspects of the grand manner, he seemed to be subverting 'civilized' values even further by dragging *art* itself (as *art* was understood by the traditionalists) down to the level of the 'vile multitude' (*canaille*), the numbed state of these lowest of all labourers, whose entire working life from youth to old age – as exemplified in the painting – was spent in backbreaking drudgery, seemingly with no redeeming spiritual or intellectual significance.

You have already looked at a nearly contemporary English painting, Ford Madox Brown's *Work* and you will consider it again in the second half of the course. You may wish then not only to compare the iconography of *Work* and *The Stonebreakers*, but also to analyse the pictorial means by which Madox

Brown achieves his aim of heroizing labour, notably the pose of the navvy who is shown standing upright and in profile for our admiration (Units 20–21, Section 3.2; Colour plate 29).

Genre was, during the period in which the academic hierarchy prevailed, the lowest of those genres which deal explicitly with the depiction of human beings and human activities. It is also, of these, the pictorial category in which the depiction of non-human motifs plays the largest part: landscape as the setting of rural labour and pastimes, still life in the representation of interior and urban crafts and professions. It is only a matter of emphasis whether a painting depicting peasants working in a field is classified as landscape or *genre*. In either case, it is no longer acceptable to regard such subjects as having a lowly status. The next genres in the traditional classification of representational pictorial art deal directly with these subjects, *landscape* and *still life*, and it is to these that we will now turn.

10 LANDSCAPE AND STILL LIFE

It's probable that you already have quite vivid ideas about these pictorial categories. Indeed, reproductions or original paintings and prints of outdoor scenery and of everyday objects (be they arrangements of flowers or foodstuffs, tableware, books, musical instruments, smoking implements, or a mixture of some or all of these) remain the best-known and loved forms of private art, or domestic pictorial decoration. Albeit low in the academic hierarchy of the genres, they have steadily gained in esteem since their revival in the sixteenth century with the rise of private collecting and under the influence of ancient texts demonstrating their popularity among Graeco-Roman connoisseurs. With some exceptions, landscapes and still lifes can be, and have been, painted for the market rather than having to wait for commissions, as must portraits of private individuals. The ideological and intellectual demands which they make on viewers are limited and flexible. Many kinds of readings (interpretations) are possible for every sub-category of landscape (some are indicated below); at the same time, we are usually able to enjoy the genre without any conscious intellectual effort.

A symbolic form of still life, called the *vanitas* or *vanity* still life (from Ecclesiastes, 1:2, 'Vanity of vanities, saith the preacher [...] all is vanity') was evolved in the Dutch university town of Leiden in the early seventeenth century (Colour plate 10). The message of pictures like this is the transience and vanity of human life, signalled here by the skull, a reminder of death, and the chronometer, reminder of the passing of time. All the other objects contribute to the theme: books symbolizing vain human knowledge, musical instruments the fleeting pleasures of the senses; the rare, collectable sea shell representing wealth, the sword, military power, and the dying lamp alluding once again to transience and frailty. But for every still life of this kind, requiring familiarity with biblical metaphor, emblem books (see p.48) and the exhortations of preachers, there have been hundreds, thousands, of others which can be enjoyed primarily for their mimetic powers, describing, for example, exotic seashells without moralizing overtones (Plate 28). Some art historians have suggested that the butterflies in this image symbolize the life of the soul free of earthly desires, but we may question whether all viewers read the painting in this way. Nor are we compelled to think of the fragility of flowers when admiring the way a painter has captured their summer vigour (Plate 29) – although we are free to do so. And when we admire the plentiful foodstuffs, gleaming glass, pewter and damask linen, the precarious balance of a plate and a knife in a picture like Plate 30, we are not forced to brood over the fate of whoever it was who absented himself so suddenly from the table. For many still-life artists, technical virtuosity was the principal ambition.

For all these reasons – production for the market rather than only on commission, popular appeal and accessibility to many different kinds of viewers – both landscapes and still lifes became the province of specialists, and lent themselves in turn to experimentation and further subdivision into specialist forms (as indeed did *genre* painting). You will readily be able to think of some of the best known types of 'landscape', such as *marine painting* or seascape, first developed by the seafaring Dutch (Plates 31 and 32); the *woodland scene* (illustrations 248, 250 and 251 in *Art and Illusion*) and even that seeming contradiction, the *townscape* (Plate 33; illustration 256 in *Art and Illusion*). Many other forms of landscape painting were evolved in response to local requirements, or in anticipation of them. The seventeenth-century Dutch painter Avercamp, for example, created the landscape of winter sports

(Plate 34) – a patriotic form, in which his countrymen, newly emancipated from Spanish rule, could recognize not only their own characteristic countryside but also themselves at play. Here *genre* and landscape are conflated (combined). In England, the landed gentry turned to landscape specialists for a commissioned form, the country house portrait. Constable's *Wivenhoe Park* (colour illustration I in *Art and Illusion*) is a late and famous example. Before Constable, Gainsborough, an artist devoted to landscape painting but starting to make his living in the 'higher' category of portraiture, conflated the two genres in a series of pictures painted in Suffolk, of which *Mr and Mrs Andrews* (Colour plate 11) is the most successful and famous. The combination of a small-scale full-length group portrait, called in England the 'conversation piece' (itself a convention inspired by *genre* painting) with landscape was evidently suggested by the artist to his patrons, rather than the other way round.

The *styles* of landscape painting (their treatment of colour, light and composition), in addition to their content (the two are related) are also subject to classification. You will find a discussion and illustrations in Chapter XI of *Art and Illusion*. The epic or heroic style (also known as 'poetic'), associated in particular with the landscape paintings of Nicolas Poussin (illustration 306 in *Art and Illusion*; Colour plate 12) 'elevates' the landscape genre to the seriousness of *istoria*, albeit only on the 'gallery' scale of Poussin's own history pictures. Colour, light and composition are used to inspire grand or poetic thoughts in such paintings, rather than to provide an accurate imitation of the real world. Colour plate 12 and illustration 306 in *Art and Illusion* once formed pendants, that is, related pictures designed to be hung together. Their content identifies them as classical or poetic landscapes in that they borrow the references to classical buildings, figures and stories common in history painting. The figures in the foreground of both enact a story from Plutarch, the first-century Greek historian, of the unjust execution of a righteous Athenian general who lost his life for refusing to pander to the populace. Both pictures draw on visual references to the world of antiquity, including engraved reconstructions of classical buildings by the sixteenth-century architect, Palladio, and views of still-standing ancient temples. More than that, the composition of both paintings makes use of horizontal-and-vertical lines and planes in a manner reminiscent of classical public architecture.

An analogous situation of subdivision into specialities exists with regard to still life. We have looked at an example of the *vanitas* category, a speciality of Leiden and presumably catering to that town's scholarly university community (Colour plate 10). Virtually the entire production of the workshop of Evariste Baschenis in the northern Italian city of Bergamo consisted of arrangements of musical instruments (Plate 35). Other specialisms included sideboard pieces and paintings of dead game.

Specialization, innovation and experimentation are fostered by the 'market economy' of these pictorial genres. When Avercamp first devised his winter sports landscapes (Plate 34), or Baschenis his musical instrument still lifes (Plate 35), they were creating at one and the same time a demand and a kind of 'brand allegiance'. Widely imitated, the Baschenis workshop products, for example, remained the only 'genuine' ones, and those clients who were both prosperous and knowledgeable 'accepted no substitutes'.

11 SUMMARY OF GENERIC CLASSIFICATION

Our survey of artistic genres has, of necessity, been selective. The following points have been highlighted as the most important for our present purposes.

(a) pre–1500

As we have mainly been concerned with the religious art of the medieval period, the two categories in this period of most relevance to us are the iconic and the narrative. Within the broad category or genre *religious art*, the sub-category of iconic religious art expressed the essence of a particular sacred person. Its function was to inspire awe. Religious narrative art told a sacred or biblical story, in which it sought to involve the viewer.

(b) 1500 – the present day

In this period, iconic conventions were either abandoned or softened. The number of genres (categories of subject-matter) of art increased. The consolidation and codification of artistic genres was partly the result of the interests of collectors (as each genre brought with it specialized problems, conventions and innovations to which collectors became increasingly alert) and partly the result of the rise of the academies. The most useful, broad distinction in this period, cutting across classifications based on subject-matter, is that between public and private art. Most of the domestic or private art with which we're now familiar (landscape, *genre*, still life, small portraits) came into prominence in the sixteenth century. The distinction between 'public' and 'private' becomes, from the Renaissance onwards, an important element in our search for meaning. As you will have gathered, the term genre, used in its broadest sense of 'type', can be applied to any significant class or type of subject-matter in art. The academies of the seventeenth, eighteenth and nineteenth centuries took a much more formal approach, however, giving a generic 'label' to works of art according to the nature of their subject-matter and attributing status to artists and works on the basis of the broad hierarchy outlined below, discussed in descending order of status.

History painting (*istoria*): religious, historical or legendary narrative subjects treated in a grand, high-minded manner, based on a classical style. Public or semi-public, large-scale narratives depicting the deeds of those 'greater than ourselves': gods, saints and heroes. History painting included representations of sacred persons and allegorical or symbolic images in classical guise, such as Barry's *Grecian Harvest Home* (Plate 17).

Portraiture: This included likenesses of:
(a) the great and the powerful, often with a public function (e.g. state portraiture);
(b) the middle classes (private or public, depending on context).

Genre: depictions of everyday life, showing the deeds of people like ourselves or worse than ourselves. Varying degrees of narrative interest. Normally for private viewing.

Landscape: the depiction of outdoor scenery, including:
(a) poetic or idealized landscapes, whose function is to arouse feeling and thought in the beholder, like those of Claude Lorrain and Poussin (a conflation of landscape and history, aspiring to public status).

(b) mimetic or topographical landscapes, based on observation of the natural world and aiming to portray it faithfully. (Such paintings often have a private status.)

Still life: everyday objects; normally private/domestic, but can be more public and/or elevated if containing the objects associated with higher status activities (for example, the attributes of war), or allegorical messages about human life, or if part of a grand commission.

When identifying the specific genre to which a painting belongs, remember that it may be more appropriate to use two or three 'labels' than to use one. Thus, the term 'narrative' may require qualification: is the painting *history* or *genre*? Conflation (or combination) of genres is also common. Gainsborough's *Mr and Mrs Andrews* is a conflation of portrait and landscape; Poussin's *The Gathering of the Ashes of Phocion* a conflation of history and landscape. It may be obvious, in such cases, that one element predominates. In Claude Lorrain's *Landscape with Moses and the Burning Bush* (illustration 307 in *Art and Illusion*), for example, a conflation of landscape and history, the primary visual interest and the artist's priority is the depiction of the landscape. The categories or genres listed above are not necessarily self-standing: there are, for example, landscapes which are both mimetic and poetic. Remember, also, that we no longer abide by the strict system of status and hierarchy outlined above, even though we continue to classify works of art according to genre. The greater freedoms we enjoy in this respect are the consequence of various nineteenth and twentieth-century rebellions.

12 A NOTE ON GENRE IN THE VICTORIAN PERIOD

You will find many of the points made in this unit particularly applicable to Victorian painting, just as our discussion of public art forms will be useful to you when dealing with Victorian architecture and monuments. Genre painting grew in popularity throughout the period and spawned many recognizable sub-genres such as graveyard scenes and cottage interiors. The artists catering to the Victorian 'collecting classes' conflated *genre* with portraiture, *genre* with landscape, and both *genre* and landscape with the moral seriousness and didactic intentions of religious narrative, the *istoria*. This led to a blurring (some would say, the breaking down) of many of the generic distinctions established by the academies.

The Pre-Raphaelites, keen in the early stages of their movement to strengthen the association between everyday life, religion and moral seriousness in their art, reacted against traditional expectations that a mimetic mode should be reserved for genre paintings and other, lower genres and that religious and historical subjects should be treated in the grand manner. Madox Brown, closely associated with the Brotherhood, wanted to make *The Last of England* (Colour plate 24) as realistic as possible: 'Absolutely without regard to the art of any period or country, I have tried to render this scene as it would appear'. (It took him four weeks to paint the red ribbons on the bonnet.) At the same time, however, he wanted to imbue the scene with the moral gravity traditionally associated with the history genre. The painting has been interpreted as a secular version of the Christian Holy Family's Flight into Egypt to escape King Herod's threat to massacre all new-born male infants. It also, of course, dealt with an event of some historical importance (see the quotation below). In such paintings, the traditional distinction between the singular and the everyday becomes blurred:

> [...] the picture is, in the strictest sense, historical. It treats of the great Emigration movement which attained its culminating point in 1865 [...] I have, in order to present the parting scene in its fullest tragic development, singled out a couple from the middle classes, high enough through education and refinement to appreciate all that they are now giving up [...] The husband broods bitterly over blighted hopes and severance from all that he has been striving for [...] (Madox Brown, quoted in C. Wood, *The Pre-Raphaelites*, p.48)

In Units 20–21 you will learn how Millais' *Christ in the Carpenter's Shop* shocked critics and public in applying a realistic style and method of depiction more normally associated with genre subjects to a religious subject (p.55). (Compare the discussion of Caravaggio, pp.73–4.) This deliberate confrontation with conventional expectations of the different genres was, for the Pre-Raphaelites, part of their spiritual war with society and a deliberate attempt to prompt viewers to derive particular meanings from their work.

Genre subjects were very popular with the Victorians, as was the symbolic use of still-life motifs in narrative paintings generally. Until the recent critical rehabilitation of Victorian art, many of these devices were reviled as 'literary', relying more on verbal discourse than on pictorial values. The two are, however, intertwined: pictorial values themselves rely on learned discrimination, tradition and convention.

Certain genres acquired new prominence in the Victorian era. The vogue for historicism led, for example, to a taste for scenes from the life of the past which, in spite of their historical flavour, had little of the heroism or moral grandeur associated with the history genre. Their narrative function relates to typical or everyday scenes from life in the past: they are a kind of conflation of history and genre. Such subjects were often valued for their exotic appeal and are often described as *historical genre* or as *subject pictures*. A good example is *The Babylonian Marriage Market* (1875) by Edwin Longsden Long, in the gallery at Royal Holloway College: the painting depicts the Babylonian custom of auctioning young women in order of their attractiveness.

The growing popularity of private art forms in the Victorian era had far-reaching consequences. Unlike the public art forms, with their requirement of communal and emphatic messages, 'lower' private art, in its ideological flexibility, also lends itself to formal experimentation of a more individualistic kind. As dealers and more sophisticated collectors came to accept 'art for art's sake' (or art preoccupied with its own formal possibilities, irrespective of its connection with life), so the literary and moral narratives dear to the Victorian public fell into disfavour; with the popularization of photography, mimesis itself lost popular esteem.

Methods of asserting the public status of a work of art diversified in the Victorian period, as *genre* paintings such as Frith's *Railway Station* (Colour Plate 53), commissioned by an art dealer, gained popularity by 'touring' a number of locations to which ticket-holders were admitted. Other paintings were circulated widely in print.

You should find that generic classification (classifying works of art according to genre) enhances your appreciation of Victorian art and assists you in discovering the various meanings to be derived from it by viewers in different periods.

Unit 12

STYLE, REPRESENTATION AND *ART AND ILLUSION*

1 CLASSIFYING ART: STYLE

Most of your work on this unit consists of a guided reading of sections of Gombrich's *Art and Illusion*, your set book. In order to derive the maximum benefit from this reading, however, you will require some preliminary discussion of the concepts of *style* and *representation*.

In Section 3.1 of Unit 11 style was defined as 'the way in which formal elements are characteristically handled by a particular artist or group of artists'. Style is the *way* in which an artist handles colour, shape and space. This may be influenced by genre. A history painter, for example, may strive for a more complex composition than that of a portrait painter, but may be less interested in a mimetic approach to colour, light and shape. Style is certainly a reflection of an artist's priorities. Most of us are familiar with the 'Impressionist style', typified by the application of paint in small touches of pure colour. This was a result of artists' desire to capture the (sometimes fleeting) effects of colour and light observable in reality. This style crossed the boundaries of the genres and was pursued in landscapes, portraits and genre subjects. Another example is the Rococo style which was popular in the eighteenth century and was 'typified by asymmetry, the use of florid s-curves and c-scrolls, and of naturalistic motifs derived from rocks, shells and plants' (Lucie-Smith, *Dictionary of Art Terms,* p.162). It was applied to history paintings and portraits, as well as to schemes of interior decoration. The preoccupation here was with decorative playfulness.

A painting classified by genre as a *portrait* might be executed in any one of a number of styles: Impressionist, Rococo, Baroque, etc. However, we've already seen that, in the eyes of the academies and of the viewing public, there was a strong association between style and genre, which continued well into the nineteenth century: Millais' application of a naturalistic Pre-Raphaelite style to a religious subject was frowned upon (see *Christ in the Carpenter's Shop*, Colour plate 21).

Gombrich's *Art and Illusion* is concerned with the ways in which different artistic styles have developed. The most common schemes of classification employed by art historians have focused on the visual appearance of art products. *Style* is the word normally used to describe 'family resemblances' which we discern in the appearance of art objects, notably but not exclusively in their formal elements and organization. It is a notoriously slippery word, since 'family resemblances' in the visual arts can be of different kinds. If you turn to *Art* and *Illusion,* illustrations 199–204, for example, you should perceive a similarity of appearance in the images reproduced in these illustrations. They are all examples of the work of one artist, the contemporary American humorist Saul Steinberg. Having looked carefully at these drawings, you would probably recognize other drawings in Steinberg's highly individual manner. We can call the 'family resemblance' discernible in all this artist's work Steinberg's 'style'. Similarly, loosely defined forms, swirling rhythms and an expressive use of colour are characteristic of Van Gogh's 'style' (*Art and Illusion,* illustration 205). Illustration 229 in *Art and Illusion* reproduces a painting by the French painter Braque, and illustration 230 one by Pablo Picasso, a Spaniard long resident in France. An expert in the work of these artists would probably be able to attribute the uncaptioned illustrations correctly, but most viewers might confuse their authorship, while perceiving a 'family resemblance' between the two. Indeed, as reading the discussion of these paintings in *Art and Illusion* will tell you, the artistic aims accountable for the appearance of these pictures, irrespective of their subject-matter, were shared by a number of artists. 'Cubism' is the name we give to the 'style' of this group or 'movement'. *Style*, then, can help us to identify a work of art as the product of a particular individual, or of one of a group, movement or school of artists.

Now turn to illustrations 104 and 60 in *Art and Illusion*. Number 104 reproduces an illustration from a Chinese manual of painting; illustration 60 shows a landscape painted in 1936 by an artist trained in the methods expounded in this seventeenth-century treatise. An expert in Chinese art would surely recognize this work as a product of the twentieth-century; to our eyes, however, its affinity with older Chinese paintings is stronger than its resemblance to the twentieth-century works with which we are familiar in the West. We would probably classify it as a picture in the 'Chinese style'.

Illustrations 82 and 83 in *Art and Illusion* reproduce two statues which, to art historians, clearly reveal their origins in ancient Greece. This is equally true of the sculpture in illustration 84; the subtle differences in the styles exemplified in these works have given rise, however, to different descriptive terms: we speak of an 'Archaic Greek style' (82, 83) and the 'Early Classical Greek style' (84). These terms refer to conventional periods in Greek history as well as to the visual characteristics of Greek art – archaeologists agree that the Archaic period 'began' at about 720 BC, and the Classical at about 480 BC.

Yet another complication in the art-historical use of the term 'style' can be demonstrated by illustration 305 in *Art and Illusion*. As you can see from the caption, this reproduces a plate from a sixteenth-century treatise on architecture. Different types of columns and their bases and capitals are depicted, all of them related to the 'orders' or types of ancient architecture. While ancient art and architecture are conventionally divided into distinctive styles – Archaic and Classical among them, as we have just seen – later art, and most especially architecture, which makes use of elements derived from ancient art, or in some way tries to recapture the 'look' of ancient art, is termed 'classical' (or 'classicizing'). As much today as in the sixteenth-century when Vignola compiled his treatise, an architect employing the ancient orders – types of columns, pedestals, capitals, cornices, etc. – will be said to be creating a building in the 'classical style'.

As you will gather from all this, categorizing art objects by style is a complex process. The concept of style may refer to characteristics of the work of a single artist, or of a grouping of artists. The latter might be united by a shared approach to the treatment of formal elements of a very conscious, deliberate kind, like those of the Cubists (illustrations 229 and 230 in *Art and Illusion*), or by the more tenuous links of a common training and culture, such as we might deduce of the Greek sculptors of the Archaic period (illustrations 82 and 83 in *Art and Illusion*). But a 'family resemblance' or style might be invoked also to group much broader families of art objects: all Western art, or all Western art harking back to the formal priorities and aims of artists of ancient Greece and Rome; all Chinese art, or all art under the influence of the formal priorities and aims of Chinese artists; all art produced in a single period (how 'periods' are to be defined in history is itself a problem).

These complexities are illustrated in the style labels most commonly used by art historians. You will have probably seen surveys of art entitled something like *Romanesque to Romantic*. These are meant to be chronologically ordered histories, implying an orderly progression from earlier styles, Romanesque in the eleventh and twelfth centuries, Gothic in the thirteenth century, Early and High Renaissance from the fifteenth to the mid-sixteenth century, to later ones, such as those labelled Neo-Classical (the eighteenth-century version of Classical) and Romantic in the nineteenth century. This kind of classification fits at least some of the observable facts. Illustrations 44 and 46 in *Art and Illusion*, for example, reproduce photographs of two French cathedrals in the Gothic style. Employing building techniques developed earlier, such as pointed (or *ogive*) arches, circular windows with stone tracery, exterior buttressing of walls to distribute weight, these constructions testify to new, shared artistic aims and provide a similar experience: a sense of organic growth upwards, rational disposition of space and volume, and, inside, maximum light and a rhythmic progression from the entrance to the space around the main altar. The Gothic style evolved in and around Paris, the capital of the French monarchy, from the elements of the earlier style, Romanesque, and it captured the imagination of church builders throughout Western Europe. In this instance, an orderly evolution of one style into another might be deduced, although, as any traveller will know, there are many local variants of Gothic, responding not only to local conditions (such as the intensity of light in Mediterranean countries as compared with the north of France), but also to formal preferences grounded in local traditions.

But the relative degree of homogeneity of Gothic is rare in the history of art, even when we limit ourselves to the art and architecture of Western Europe. In most periods, local needs and traditions actually 'win out' over international trends. Thus most art-historical surveys supplement their schemes of classifying through period style labels (Romanesque, Gothic, etc.) with schemes of classification based on national or local variations. These categories both overlap and leave unexplored gaps. A specialist might infer that when the 'Venetian school' is mentioned in a general survey, discussion will probably centre on Venetian sixteenth-century painting in the High Renaissance style, of which Titian is a major exponent (Colour plate 1); however the term might encompass also the classicizing architecture of Palladio (1518–80) and the eighteenth-century frescoes of the Tiepolo family of painters (which might also appear under the periodic style label, Rococo). 'The school of Delft', on the other hand, almost certainly will be used to refer only to the small-scale easel pictures painted in the 1650s by Carel Fabritius, Jan Vermeer and Pieter de Hooch; the periodic style label, Baroque, identified primarily with a style of Italianate architecture, sculpture and large-scale painting of the seventeenth century, sits uneasily with the products of the Delft school.

The skill of classifying works of art according to style is one which is acquired over time. You will develop it as you proceed with your studies on this and other courses. The definition of style labels (for example, 'What do we mean by 'Baroque'?) need not concern us at the moment. Ultimately, however, students of art history find it useful to be able to recognize the 'family resemblances' indicated by the style labels commonly in use, at least roughly to date and place art products, and to recognize the individual styles of the best-known artists.

2 REPRESENTATION

Some key terms

Representation and *representational* are commonly used to imply 'resemblance' or 'likeness'. However, the terms are also used by art historians in more specialized ways. To *represent* is used to describe the *process* by which the visible world, or ideas, or states of mind, are rendered in a work of art. A work of art which attempts to establish a resemblance or imitation of a reality in the external world can be said to be representing that reality. But this representation is, of course, not the same as the thing itself, it is a codification of it according to the conventions of painting. It follows from this that an object from the real world can be successfully represented in a painting without it being necessary for the artist to establish a close resemblance to it in paint. A painting can represent the real world by referring to it, not only by establishing a likeness to it. Look again at Braque's *Still Life: The Table (Art and Illusion,* illustration 229). It has a title which suggests that it refers to, or represents, a common object in the world. The information available to you is limited because it is reproduced in black and white, but it is clear that while objects like the guitar, apples, a jug, a napkin, etc. are clearly decipherable on a table top, we would not claim that they had any high degree of likeness to any of these things that we had seen. These objects are represented according to the style, or conventions, of Cubism. But what about the objects illustrated in Plates 2, 3 and 4 of the *Illustration booklet?* Can they be called representational? They do not seek to resemble or refer to some object external to themselves. However, they could be said to *represent* the ideas of the artist in a visual form. Some abstract artists would claim that their paintings represent, or *express,* emotions or spiritual states of mind, or abstract ideas (such as truth, chaos, the essence of art itself).

At this stage it is important for you to understand *representation* as a process in art whereby certain things (for example, bowls of apples, actual people) are *presented* again – re-presented – not in their original constituents of three-dimensional fruit, or flesh and blood, but in pigments on a flat canvas. When you think of representation, try to think of it as *re-presentation,* recasting, transforming, transposing, providing a coded equivalent, *not* reflecting, mirroring, recording. This re-presentation can take a number of forms according to varying conventions. The following terms are frequently used in describing works of art. They can indicate different *degrees* of resemblance of works of art to the objects they are representing. It is important to recognize that these are not hard and fast definitions. There are overlaps between the terms and different writers may use them with a different emphasis.

Mimetic. As we have already seen (p.73) a mimetic work is one which attempts a close degree of imitation of or of resemblance to the object(s) it represents.

Naturalistic is a fairly imprecise term, used to refer to art which has a high degree of resemblance, particularly to the surface properties of the objects represented: colours, textures, the way light is reflected. It also often implies that the image conveys 'the unvarnished truth', or, by extension, that a squalid or ugly aspect of the natural or man-made world is conveyed.

Illusionism is generally used to refer to such a *high* degree of resemblance that the representation gives the viewer the illusion – at least for a moment – of being that which it represents. A ceiling painted to look like an opening onto the sky is said to be *illusionistic. Trompe l'œil* (French for 'deceive the eye') is a strong term for illusionistic representation. It is most often used for a kind of painting or sculpture in which the image is used as a substitute for the object depicted – a cupboard door, for example, painted to look like the contents of the cupboard – and tends to imply parity of scale between the image and the object depicted. So, for example, a *trompe l'œil* image of a shelf full of books will be of the same size as an actual shelf of books, the better to deceive the eye of the beholder.

Another term useful for our present purposes is:

Figurative; this is used to describe any art which represents, in however altered or distorted a form, motifs, objects and figures perceived in the visible world.

2.1 *ART AND ILLUSION* AND REPRESENTATION

In his inquiry into the process of representation (of how artists strive to make works constructed from paint, marble, etc. resemble or refer to aspects of the visible world), Gombrich is naturally pre-occupied with style, since style is 'the way a picture looks', the way in which formal elements are handled by the artist. Style is therefore a *means* of representation and, as discussed in the previous section, can vary enormously in character (or *mode*) from one artist to another, from one period or region to another. One of the aims of these units is to introduce you to a wide range of art, rather than to concentrate on the art of a narrow historical period. The point of getting you to look at this range of material is not that you should end up with a detailed knowledge of a chronology of Western art, but that you should be aware of this diversity and of how certain problems are raised by it. 'Problems', to stress a point, are not of the kind that should depress us! 'Problems', in the sense of the term used here, are the interesting issues that need clarifying: attending to these can help us to see why works of art look the way they do.

Because Gombrich's book is about the problems of representation, *Art and Illusion* is organized not chronologically but thematically: the chapter headings show you that he is taking us through an argument, not giving us a survey of art from the very beginning. How then, you may ask, can we be expected to understand his argument *about* art when we do not first know the history? How can we think about representation and interpretation before we are familiar with what happened when? Well, the first point to make is that to chronicle changes in art is not as simple as it may first appear; any survey is in fact a particular interpretation of history. And, in interpreting, we make assumptions, based on our own views of what art is, or should be. The problem is that interpretations of works of art are never fixed; they change over time. This is a positive argument for looking at how representation works and how meanings are constructed in art *as we learn about art*, not as an after-thought. Secondly, although *Art and Illusion* is a book about representation, and why representation should be seen to have a history, it is not suggesting simply a progressive history of styles. Gombrich devises various categories to explain why art looks different at different times (such as changing 'schemata' and 'mental sets', terms which are glossed below). The whole point of these categories is to show to be false the view of representational art as a mirror, in which nature is reflected more and more perfectly as times goes on. Gombrich's aim is to show that artists do not passively 'copy' nature, but that artists of any period depend on previously established conventions. It's plain that (a) a bowl of fruit and (b) a painting of a bowl of fruit are entirely different objects. We are able to forge a connection between them, however, because of our immersion in the powerful conventions governing the ways in which particular configurations of pigment on canvas can re-present or signify to us objects in the visible world. It follows that an understanding of the art of particular historical periods (such as you will study in the interdisciplinary part of the course on Britain between 1850 and 1890) is possible only in the light of some knowledge of those conventions.

'Convention' is a term which you will find used frequently in your units and in *Art and Illusion*. It is an important term in the language of art history and means an established method: in painting, for instance, a traditional way of representing the three-dimensional world on a two-dimensional canvas. Artists work with traditions which are constantly changing. To stress this aspect of the artistic process, as Gombrich does, has important implications. If artists work with conventions, then art is not simply spontaneous self-expression, uninfluenced by culture or history. The idea of art as the creative out-pouring of an individual genius is a commonly held belief, which Gombrich challenges by asking us to think of art as a much more complex activity. (It may be that Gombrich's experience of Nazi Germany made him see individual genius as anarchic and destructive.)

Having spelt out the positive aspects of *Art and Illusion* as a set text, let us try to set your mind at rest about possible problems you might have. *Any* book will pose some; in this case the length of the book, its density in parts and the number of names with which you won't be familiar (there's no reason why you should be) might daunt you to begin with. So the first thing to get clear is that you should not worry about retaining every detail of the book. It's the sort of book that can be taken on many levels, and on a first reading we would not expect you to understand its most sophisticated aspects. The guide below is intended to help you follow the main arguments as you read the book and to understand key points – that is what matters, not what Gombrich thinks about another commentator's position. Do not get caught up in the references to other writers in Gombrich's texts, but try to keep in mind the idea he is pursuing. The ideas that Gombrich puts forward in this book can change the whole way we think about visual things – because he addresses directly many of the assumptions and preconceptions we have about visual art. In that sense it's not a book we should read after years of study, but right at the start – why allow our preconceptions to inform our view of art unnecessarily?

3 GUIDED READING OF *ART AND ILLUSION*

We'll now look at various sections of *Art and Illusion* together, so that you can follow some of Gombrich's main arguments. In order to make this task manageable you will be set a series of exercises in which you will be directed to read specific extracts. After reading the extracts, consider the following discussions which comment on and amplify Gombrich's points. If you find that you are intrigued by the drift of Gombrich's argument at any point, please read on beyond the specified extracts. As you will see, selected parts of the Introduction and Chapters 1–5 are required reading: the rest of the book is *optional*. The most enjoyable aspect of Gombrich's work is the way in which he allows illustrations to do some of his arguing for him. Please do not skip these, as they are reinforcements and demonstrations of his points about perception and art. As we look at Gombrich's ideas, we'll indicate the ways in which they develop or extend some of the approaches to art history we've met in previous sections of these units. (You will find that Gombrich consistently uses gendered language; this was common style at the time when *Art and Illusion* was first published.)

Exercise

Read section 1 of Gombrich's Introduction, pp. 3–4.

Discussion

The 'riddle of style' is Gombrich's starting point: why does art in different periods and in different cultures look different? Why are medieval artistic representations of trees, humans, birds and rivers different from twentieth century representations, even when the objects themselves have not changed substantially? Given the enormous range of images we encounter, what is it that accounts for one 'style' or another? By 'style', Gombrich means the way the picture looks, the particular characteristics of an artist's treatment of formal elements or of re-presenting the visible world. Because of the range of art on which he focuses, Gombrich is mainly concerned with representation of the visible world. He does also consider, however, representation of states of mind (in Chapter XI). He refers to the latter process as *expression*, thus distinguishing it from mimetic representation, which is concerned with the world of visible appearances. Use of the term *expression* also relates to other aspects of artistic activity, principally the role of emotion in the creative process.

Note what Gombrich has to say in the first couple of paragraphs in this section. He uses Alain's cartoon of the Egyptian life class to pose the problem of the 'riddle of style' – why modes of representing are so diverse. The joke plays on the incompatibility of the highly stylized manner of Egyptian art, which probably fails to represent faithfully the way Egyptians looked in reality, and the very different purpose of the life class, to paint 'nature' faithfully, which is often taken to be the standard against which all art is judged. Gombrich makes the point (p.3) that the job of the art historian has traditionally been to describe the changes that have taken place in art, rather than to explain why 'not everything is possible in every period', as the German art historian Wölffin had put it (p.4). This needs a little explanation since the kind of art history you are studying in these units does not just consist of describing changes in art. This is because art history as a discipline has changed since Gombrich was writing in the late fifties. Indeed, many of Gombrich's concerns in *Art and Illusion* have been assimilated into the study of art history, which gives you some idea of the influence his book has had. Art historians *are* now concerned not only with chronicling the changes in artistic style which have taken place over the centuries (which style came after which), but also with asking why certain styles arise (or fail to arise) – what factors facilitated or prohibited the growth of different styles at certain times, in certain places and societies. They have responded to Gombrich's challenge, '... whose business is it?', by asking *why* different ages and nations have represented the visible world in such different ways.

Gombrich goes on in the Introduction to discuss the quest in art for mimesis, for a close resemblance to the visible world. Earlier, in his preface (p.xi) he states that the real purpose of *Art and Illusion* is 'to explain the reasons for the unexpected difficulty which artists encountered who clearly wanted to make their images look like nature'. He feels at the time of writing that the problems of representation have been underestimated by art historians: they have failed to appreciate the difficulties faced by artists in the past who tried to 'imitate' or reflect the visible world. He suggests that his colleagues have failed to explore the complexities involved in the idea of 'painting what you see', because they have not fully understood that seeing is conditioned or shaped by pre-existing knowledge: the work of our eyes is influenced by the knowledge stored in our brain. Those who fail to explore the implications of this are particularly remiss, suggests Gombrich, because thinkers active as long ago as the Roman, Pliny (of the first century AD), had emphasized the fact that the stored knowledge and memories of the mind influence the way in which we perceive or see the world. Thus, it is reasonable to suppose that artists, when translating what they 'see' onto canvas, will be influenced by deep (even subconscious?) memories of, for example, the way these objects felt when they touched them. Artists will also call on the conventions and formulae used by preceding artists who strove to represent the same objects or effects. What is at issue here is the *psychology* of pictorial representation.

'The Limits of Likeness' is the title of the whole of Part One of the book, comprising the first two chapters 'From light into paint' and 'Truth and the stereotype'. Art is often assumed to be a matter of simply 'copying' the visible world, but Gombrich contests this assumption. He shows that art which seems to resemble the world, does so because it represents it convincingly: it is a matter of *re-presentation*, of actively re-presenting the world in a picture. That is, a picture must give us sufficient clues, through the medium of paint, to identify or describe the objects it seeks to represent. This, in turn, rests on an underlying (and conventional) assumption that pigment on canvas *can* signify real things out in the world. Always remember that paintings actually resemble other paintings – as two-dimensional flat objects – more than they resemble the three-dimensional world they may represent. Thus the artist 'cannot transcribe what he sees; he can only translate it into the terms of his medium' (p.30); it is translated into a type of 'code' (p.34). Not everything is possible at any one time, and the limitations and constraints imposed vary in different periods (such limitations as medium, for example). Working in pencil or oil will make different requirements of artists working in the same period (or even of a single artist, such as Constable, see p.33).

Exercise

Read Chapter 1 of *Art and Illusion*, *'From light into paint'*, p.29 to the bottom of p.39.

Discussion

From what you have read so far, it is obvious that Gombrich is concerned with the different conventions artists have developed in their use of light and shade (a) to distinguish between figure and ground (the background against which we see a figure) and (b) to suggest three dimensions. (On shadow modelling, see above, pp.24 and 61.) Tonal gradations (see above, p.24), the 'more' or 'less' of light, have been central to this experimentation. Gombrich now goes on to discuss the specific nature of Constable's experiment: how to reconcile local colour (the colour inherent in a particular object, irrespective of surrounding influences such as shadows and reflections) with the range of tonal gradations needed to suggest depth in the 'code' of art. Constable's experiments are seen in relation to those of his predecessor, the seventeenth-century landscape artist, Claude Lorrain.

Exercise

Read pp.40–2 (to '... not a copy').

Discussion

The Claude glass was a contraption (a kind of compact, tinted mirror) used by landscape artists in the eighteenth century and named after the effects created by the seventeenth-century artist Claude Lorrain. It reduced the glare from brightly lit surfaces, thus allowing the viewer who reflected the view of a particular terrain in it to see the whole scene in a reduced light. In other words, it distorted colours (made them 'browner') so that the bright colours of an actual scene could be more successfully harmonized with all of its other colours: what was emphasized was their *tonal* value rather than their hue. This allowed artists to see how light or tonal values could be used to convey a sense of distance. (See above, p.28, on aerial perspective, of which Claude was a skilful practitioner.) What Constable was looking for was a more faithful rendering of the hues he observed in nature, while maintaining the usefulness of tonal values in suggesting depth. Even Constable's greens, however, were not the greens of the real scene he strove to represent: art can only transpose; it cannot copy.

Gombrich's whole book is about the problem of 'representation' and why representation should be seen to have a history. Note here, though, that by rejecting art as the 'transcription' of reality, Gombrich stresses the process of representation as an activity dominated by *conventions*, with which both artist and viewer are familiar. By 'means of representation' is meant those formal devices and techniques which the artist uses to suggest, for example, that space recedes in the picture (when literally it is a flat canvas), that light falls on a figure (when literally the 'light' is a painted surface), that we are looking down on a scene (when the artist has selected this particular viewpoint to paint). The vital point is that representation is a recasting, providing a coded equivalent, an active not a passive process (see above, pp.86 and 90). As we shall see as we read more of Gombrich's book, not only is this an active process for the artist making a representation, but also for the spectator who actively 'reads' the picture (Gombrich calls this 'the beholder's share'; see below).

Exercise

Read pp.42–6 (to the end of Section II).

Discussion

Gombrich declares that the 'truth of a landscape painting is relative' (p.43). Working in different historical periods will impose different requirements of a 'likeness' or of an accurate representation. Since there is no one standard of 'likeness', it follows that how convincing any painting, say a landscape, is, is *relative* to other representations of landscape: we make our judgements according to our experience of how landscape has normally been represented.

If the artist is influenced by such memories and conventions, so is the spectator (or beholder). The artist must have an understanding of the beholder's ability to register and interpret the tonal relationships within a painting. This ability allows us to 'decode' an artist's use of light, even where the colours used do not match perfectly those of the original: think of our responses to black-and-white images. It is the internal *relationships* in a painting (e.g. between light and dark) which render it convincing to us.

Exercise

Read pp.46–50.

Discussion

Having established the fact that different generations have different expectations of the intensity and relationships of light and dark which constitute an effective representation of a scene (the Impressionists first 'dazzled' viewers), Gombrich explains further the importance of convention, expectation and innovation in the process of representation.

Exercise

Read pp.51–4.

Discussion

A 'mental set' is a conceptual framework; by it, Gombrich refers to *habits* of seeing, representing and interpreting. This idea, that art has to do with the habits of mind, however various, within a given culture and historical period, is in conflict with the idea of art as the sole creation of a single individual governed only by his or her supposedly unique vision. It follows that if art is produced within different 'mental sets' at different periods, then art of the past will not automatically mean the same to us now, with our different habits of mind. For Gombrich it is historical imagination which can make the art of other periods accessible to us: it becomes accessible if we can make the right adjustments (and that is what we try to do when we study art history). Both artist and beholder are influenced by a 'mental set', or the habits of mind typical of a particular period. This is why Constable's starting point for his experiment was Claudian conventions and why, when he broke free of those conventions, he produced a shock. In an earlier passage (pp.24–5) Gombrich emphasizes that art has a history *because* the illusions (or representations) created by art are not only the product but the indispensable *tools* for the artist's analysis of appearances: far from relying on a 'genius' which is free from constraints, an artist depends upon the conventions or 'codes' used by preceding artists and which are familiar to viewers. The concept of 'mental set' helps us to understand how, for example, the Victorian art establishment could be so shocked by the Pre-Raphaelites. It also explains why social and cultural history are essential components of art history: we must understand the particular habits of mind common among artists and public at the time a particular work was produced. Only in this way can we place a particular artist's attempts at representation within contexts of convention, expectation, experimentation and innovation. Gombrich focuses on conventions and developments *within* the art world, but in the second half of the course you will have the opportunity to see how a broader survey of a society and of its 'habits of mind' (Victorian, in our case) can illuminate the expectations, traditions and representational efforts of its artists.

In Chapter II, 'Truth and the stereotype', Gombrich refers again to the limits of artistic transcription of the world. He returns to the question of why it is that paintings vary so considerably in style, even when artists share the common objective of mimesis.

Exercise

Read pp.55–8 (to the end of Section I).

Discussion

Gombrich raises the question of the relationship between reality and the 'objectivity' (faithfulness to reality) or mimetic qualities of a work. He goes on to discuss how we should proceed in our discussions of pictorial objectivity or 'truth'.

Exercise

Read pp.58–63 (to '... bad for the information').

Discussion

A painting cannot be true or false like a statement (Gombrich explains this on p.59), but we can be convinced by an image because it builds on familiar representations to show us the unfamiliar. The idea here is that rather than the real world being the measure of a painting's 'truthfulness', the measure we apply is actually a comparison with other visual representations, or paintings. At this point, Gombrich calls these familiar ways of representing a 'stereotype', a pre-conceived pattern. This pre-conceived pattern is not an obstacle to representation, but a necessary part of it.

On page 62 Gombrich introduces the term *schema* (plural schemata). The schema, like the stereotype, is the basic set of conventions with which the artist necessarily works. Through observation and experience, the schema is adjusted, adapted or 'corrected'. Schemata, then, are the particular conventions or established techniques for representing the world. Both *schema* and *schemata* are fairly elastic concepts. They can refer to the very minimum for representing, say, a head, the oval or egg-shape (see *Art and Illusion* pp.144–6), or any other motif (e.g. a castle), or to an established artistic convention relating to a compositional technique or to the use of light. Two of the *schemata* derived by artists from Claude Lorrain's paintings were the use of trees to 'frame' the landscape and suggest recession and the use of tonal gradations to suggest distance. As we've seen, the latter *schema* was adopted and 'corrected' by Constable. When an artist attempts to 'copy' an object or scene from the real world (s)he is bound to classify the shape or the effect in accordance with a familiar schema. As Gombrich goes on to say in the rest of this section, the schema is the 'first, approximate, loose category which is gradually tightened to fit the form it is to reproduce'. In drawing or designing, artists seek approximations to the schemata and patterns they have learned to handle.

Exercise

Read section III, pp.64–7.

Discussion

The schema, then, is not derived from the portion or object of the world that is being represented, but is the familiar set of conventions with which the artist approaches the model or the visible world. The artist tries to analyse the world in terms of familiar artistic motifs. This would explain why it is that artistic styles have a 'history': if artistic production is influenced by a familiarity with certain conventions and techniques, there will be a different set of possibilities for each artist or group of artists we examine. Artists tend to look for motifs or elements of the visible world for which their style and training equip them. They need a 'vocabulary' before embarking on a representation of reality.

Exercise

Read the remainder of Chapter II, to p.78.

Discussion

Gombrich here reinforces the idea that an artist's endeavours are determined by the schemata within their consciousness and which they can confidently handle. (Gombrich later relates this to the example of the way a portrait may begin as the schema of a head (an oval or egg-shape) which is then modified or 'corrected' by the addition of the distinctive features about which we need to give information, pp.142–4.) The 'truth' or 'objectivity' of the resulting image will then be judged (a) in relation to the correct information about the subject it gives us by comparison with other representations and (b) in accordance with the function attributed to the image (see pp.58–9; what do we want to *know* about the object(s) depicted?). The correct portrait, says Gombrich (p.78), is the 'end product on a long road through schema and correction': that is, the artist adapts the schema to fit the particular face of a sitter. How much a schema needs adjusting, he argues, often depends on the requirements of a particular society (see p.78).

The schema, then, does not stay still, it changes over time. The 'schema' ('framework', 'stereotype', 'convention') is an idea which incorporates as large a category as 'genre' (as in the generic categories of landscape, history painting, portraiture and so on, which we might regard as conventional *frameworks*) and as small and detailed a point as the use of 'highlight', dashes of white paint, to stand in for light. You may recall the way in which Raphael adapted the 'schema' or genre, 'domestic Madonna and child', 'half-length Madonna picture', in accordance with differing aims and priorities (see above, p.58). Much as they differ from each other, however, all three of the Madonna and Child images we examined earlier seem to depict a formulaic Madonna, a schematic child. Neither Madonna nor Child is *individualized* to any great extent, because, in the 'mental set' of the sixteenth century, such individualization would have reduced the ideals of beauty and maternal love to imperfect copies. The schematic portrayal of the Virgin asserts, in the eyes of those who share the expectations of Raphael and his contemporaries, her perfection. The ready visibility of the schema demonstrates that the image is more an *icon* than a narrative representation of a moment in the life of a young mother. In this context, a 'schematic' representation is one which conforms closely to the 'rules of the game' (see Unit 10, pp.13–14) as relevant to a given genre. As already discussed in Unit 11, the formal or stylistic elements of a painting, and the degree of correction to which a schema is subjected, depend significantly on the subject-matter and whether the role of the work is private or public.

There is no need to read Chapter III at the moment, but you will be asked to read a section of it at a later stage. The next paragraph offers a brief summary of some of the main ideas of Chapter III, which will be useful before you read Chapter IV.

In Part Two, 'Function and Form', Gombrich deals with the process of 'making and matching'. 'Making' (creating images) is a constant factor which runs through various cultures and periods, whereas 'matching' is not. 'Matching', i.e. producing art which 'matches' or seeks to resemble reality, proceeds through the process of 'schema and correction'; the greater the degree of correction, the greater the degree of matching. The more correction and matching involved, the more the art work will seem to resemble reality, and this extremely sophisticated process Gombrich sees as a great achievement in Western art. However, it is not universal (i.e. applicable to *all* art at all times). Gombrich uses the phrase, 'making before matching', which, it seems, draws a distinction between making art and making art whose aim (or function, in Gombrich's terminology) is to resemble reality. Some makers of images, argues Gombrich, were much more concerned to make (*create*) an image with a live or magical *presence* than to produce a likeness. In some types of art, portraiture, for instance, resemblance may be more important than in others. The function of a work is central to our understanding of the mode of representation it employs.

In Chapter IV Gombrich is very much concerned with a period of history in which artists *were* concerned with 'matching' or with creating a resemblance to the real world. Why, he asks, does Greek art appear so 'realistic' when viewed beside Egyptian art? The answer, he suggests, lies in a consideration of the *function* of art in each of these two cultures. Egyptian art was concerned with 'the embodiment of the typical in its most lasting and changeless form', whereas Greek art intended to tell stories. Greek art came to view individual figures not as anonymous tokens but as actors in a story, in an imagined reality. It therefore generated a different 'mental set' or set of expectations, including a striving for greater lifelikeness or for 'matching' reality. This involved ceaseless experimentation with the correction of inherited schemata. This relationship between *function* (or purpose) and form is relevant to our earlier distinctions between iconic and narrative art (see above, pp.35–41).

Before you read Chapter IV, you need to know that in Chapter III Gombrich refers to the Greek philosopher Plato's ideas on art and reality. Plato's philosophy distinguishes between reality and appearance. He argues that particular objects or forms are only appearances (or copies) of universal ideas or realities. (Thus, an individual cat is only a specific and limited embodiment, or copy, of the general, universal idea – or class – of 'cattiness'.) According to Plato, therefore, the artist who engages in mimesis (a faithful imitation of forms as they *appear* in the visible world) is attempting to make a copy of a copy (see pp.83–4 of *Art and Illusion*).

Exercise

Read Chapter IV of *Art and Illusion*. If you find the first page or two a little hard-going, skip to the paragraph beginning, 'For us, who have lived ...' on page 108. (It may be useful to know that Paris was a Trojan prince who awarded a golden apple to Venus in a contest of beauty between her, Juno and Minerva.)

Discussion

Gombrich argues that it was the 'free play of the imagination in artist and beholder alike', or a preoccupation with 'imaginative accounts of past events', which accounts for the move towards mimesis in Greek art. How can the beholder become imaginatively involved in a scene if it does not look 'convincing'? He is keen to emphasize this relationship between form and function because many commentators have attributed a more realistic (or mimetic) style in art to a closer *observation* of nature or reality on the artist's part. He refutes this by arguing that Egyptians observed nature as closely as the Greeks: their art was different because they had a different purpose in mind for it. The emergence of iconic Christian art *after* the achievements of Greek representational art further proves this point: style or mode of representation are, in large part, a product of function, not of a simple capability to look carefully at the world. (Think back to the comments made on function in Unit 10, pp.8–20 and Unit 11, p.34.)

In Chapter V, Gombrich discusses the rules (or formulae) taught in art training at different times. The ways in which these formulae are then adapted in the light of experience is an example of the more general process of representation (and of 'schema and correction', see pp.144–7). The point is not that art can be learnt by rote, but that nevertheless the artist uses certain skills which are internalized as conventions. (And, as you know, we can internalize ideas or ways of visualizing or thinking about things consciously *or* subconsciously.) *Formula, convention* and *schema* can be used interchangeably: you should not worry about the subtler distinctions between them.

We have already seen that a *schema* can be something as narrow as the accepted, basic formula for depicting a certain shape or object (for example, a cat or a rabbit: many of us are aware of the common schemata used to depict those animals!) or as broad as a formula, framework or conventional device for approaching, say, a particular genre or subject or a compositional effect. In Chapter V Gombrich focuses on *schema* in its narrower sense. He compares a schema (basic pattern or formula) to Plato's concept of a 'universal': a *class* of things of which individuals are merely instances. (Thus an individual person is a particular instance of the general class, 'human'.) A schema (or universal) is particularized, 'corrected' or individualized by a draughtsman or woman until it resembles the individual object, form or figure he or she wishes to depict. An appropriate example of this (not discussed by Gombrich) is the Renaissance artist Filippo Lippi who corrected the schema of the classical nude in accordance with the growing anatomical knowledge of his time (Woolf and Cassin, *Bodylines*, p. 21).

Exercise

Read Chapter V, up to the end of section III (p.133).

In section IV, Gombrich goes on to describe what he sees as a relationship between Plato's ideas and the aspirations of some artists who worked between 1550 and 1850. In this period, he says, many artists adopted Plato's view that individual trees, men, cats, etc. are imperfect or distorted copies of universals, essences, or 'eternal patterns'. They became snobbish about 'mere copies' of individual, particular objects in the observable world and tried, instead, to capture their underlying structure, pattern or essence. The academies played a particularly strong role in this and encouraged what they described as the quest for 'beautiful' or 'idealized' nature. In practice, however, artists were probably influenced by conventions or schemata rather than by unattainable, universal essences. Gombrich now goes on to describe how schemata or 'conceptual' elements (ideas and images in the *mind* of the artist) influenced the teaching of drawing.

Exercise

Read sections IV, V and VI of Chapter V (pp.133–48). Gombrich refers to a 'lay figure' in this section. This is a jointed wooden manikin which can be arranged in any position and which is used by artists for the study of the proportions of the human body.

Discussion

Gombrich's point that perception is active rather than passive is crucial (pp.147–8). We do not passively 'register' what we see. On the contrary, seeing or perception is based on anticipation: we see what we expect to see and we then notice any deviations from our anticipation. This is what artists (like everybody else) do when they 'observe the world'.

Exercise

Read section VII of Chapter V.

Discussion

Gombrich discusses the way in which many artists, from the late eighteenth century onwards, professed to turn their back on conventions, schemata, and even on the search for universals evident in narrative paintings in the grand, classical manner, in order to seek their inspiration directly from nature. He argues that such professions involved self-delusion. Even artists like Constable, who try to 'see' the world directly, uninfluenced by schemata, are, in fact, influenced by tradition and convention. What Constable and his contemporaries *did* achieve, however, was the focusing of the viewer's attention on the world of nature rather than on narrative scenes of imagined reality.

The 'beholder's share' is the subject of Part Three of *Art and Illusion*, which deals with the role of the viewer or spectator in the process of representation. However, before you proceed with Part III, you should read the section of Chapter III in which Gombrich outlines the way in which viewers can 'project' familiar forms or schemata, stored in the 'filing' system of their minds, onto other shapes.

Exercise

Read section IV of Chapter III, pp.89–93.

Discussion

In Part Three, the concept of projection is extended to stress further the active role played by the viewer in 'reading' a work of visual art. If an image is ambiguous, we will select from various readings that we are led to project onto it the one which makes the most sense. Gombrich discusses how landscape paintings, for example, could be read out of various arrangements of ink blots (p.157). 'Projection' is a feature of the way we make sense of things in our everyday experience, how we perceive the world in general. Gombrich relates this psychological process to the process of representation in art.

Just as the artist has been shown to come to the practice of art with anything but an 'innocent eye', so too this is true of the viewer when he or she looks at a work of art. We look at art and understand that it is a representation if we are familiar with the conventions it uses. The process of 'checking-up' on the image, unconsciously relating it to other representations and seeing whether it is plausible, is what Gombrich identifies as 'tests of consistency' (p.196). For the viewer to be able to read the image requires what Gombrich calls the 'conditions of illusion' (the title of Chapter VII) to be right. By this, Gombrich is basically saying that the context needs to be favourable for the representation to work; some contradiction of the viewer's expectations can be accommodated, but not so much that the process of making sense of an image falls down completely. The dots and dashes of a facial schema may work only in the context of an oval face-shape; out of that context, they may just fail to register as a face. In order to be deemed successful or effective, therefore, representational art must incorporate sufficient (and consistent) familiar schemata, or visual 'clues' internalized by the spectator. This relates to the notion of 'mental set' already discussed above (pp.92–3).

At this point, we would like to offer you some options for further reading. If you have found Gombrich's ideas exciting and accessible, you may wish to read on to the end of the book. If, however, time and inclination dictate otherwise, you may prefer to *select* certain chapters or passages from Part Three in order to complete your reading of *Art and Illusion*. In either case, you should read the brief guides to each chapter, printed below. Do not, however, treat these summaries and commentaries as substitutes for reading the book itself. In most of the remaining chapters (except Chapter 9) Gombrich's arguments are clarified and come alive through the illustrations to which he refers.

Chapter VI, 'The image in the clouds'

Here, Gombrich explores the way in which the beholder is given the opportunity to 'decode' a work of art. The mind of the beholder plays an active part in representation by projecting familiar shapes or schemata onto the whole or parts of a painting. Artists can give greater scope to the beholder's imagination if their forms and compositions are 'loose', more suggestive , less precise (less 'finished'). This is the case in the preliminary sketches of Cozens, where 'making' the image takes precedence over the process of 'matching', 'correction' or mimetic detail. The artist-beholder then has the job of projecting meaning onto or interpreting the shapes or spectacle presented, in accordance with 'things or images stored in (the) mind' (an analogous situation arises when we project shapes onto burning coals). Cozens's method, 'blotting', involved 'the use of accidental inkblots for the suggestion of landscape motifs' and artists were able to interpret these 'blots' because they were already attuned to the landscape forms used by Claude Lorrain. Often, the sense which a spectator makes of such loosely painted works is related to the distance from which the paintings are viewed.

Gombrich relates this phenomenon to the distinction between a precise (linear) finish and more *painterly* works (see Unit 10, p.25). Thus, Reynolds admired the painterly portraits of Gainsborough, which were suggestive rather than precise: 'it is supposed that in this undetermined manner there is the general effect; enough to remind the spectator of the original; the imagination supplies the rest, and perhaps more satisfactorily..., if not more exactly, than the artist, with all his care, could possibly have done...'. It is Gombrich's view that this painterly manner, which involves a deal of experience of the visual hints necessary to the spectator, demands much skill. Equally, paintings of this nature demand more of the spectator, whose imagination must work harder in the search for meaning.

Chapter VII, 'Conditions of illusion'

Gombrich enters into greater detail here on the role of the beholder in projection. The beholder's knowledge and 'power to guess' are most rigorously tested by art in which 'incomplete' (i.e. blurred, hazy, ill-defined or unfinished) forms are used. Impressionist art is a case in point. Gombrich argues that the successful illusion created by Impressionist art is due, in part, to the fact that it gives us just enough hints, clues or familiar schemata to enable us to make sense of the whole or of parts of paintings. This is one of the reasons why it uses *familiar* subjects drawn from contemporary life: the beholder's knowledge of the context or situation will allow him or her to fill in any 'gaps' of interpretation, provided there are no contradictory hints in the work concerned. The beholder's projective faculty will be particularly effective at a certain distance from a work of incomplete or indeterminate forms:

> The distance from the canvas weakens the beholder's power of discrimination and creates a blur which mobilizes his projective faculty. The indistinct parts of the canvas become a screen [onto which the beholder projects form and meaning], provided only that certain distinctive features stand out with sufficient force and that no contradictory messages reach the eye to spoil the impression. (p. 186)

According to Gombrich, we, as beholders, 'probe the distant and indeterminate for possible classifications, which we then test and elaborate in a game of projections'. We make guesses and assess probabilities, where the information provided by the artist is not precise. It is our mental set or 'habits of mind' which make us ready to begin projecting and interpreting in this way. We know when our 'guesses' are wrong, because they do not pass the test of *consistency*: they are not plausible within a given context or category of experience. Gombrich argues these points through his illustrations in an entertaining way.

Chapter VIII, 'Ambiguities of the third dimension'

(Sections IV and V of this chapter are particularly difficult and you may wish to leave them to one side.) Chapter VIII focuses on the beholder's share in the reading or interpretation of spatial arrangements and looks at perspective as the most important trick in the armoury of illusionist art. Gombrich looks at the way in which perspective theory (see Unit 10, pp.27–9) can help to deceive the eye and eliminate ambiguity. Artists have developed means (such as shadow modelling and converging lines) of encouraging the beholder to read the spatial relationships within a painting in a particular way. The beholder draws on his or her knowledge and experience in order to estimate, for example, the distance between one figure and another. The beholder's 'guess' in such a situation tends to push possible ambiguities to one side, and is steered in a particular direction by contextual and mutually reinforcing clues. In the perception of spatial relationships the beholder latches onto familiar devices or signals. This method of perceiving and interpreting a representation is parallel, then, with the artist's method of proceeding, as it involves a sequence of schema (recognizable conventions) and correction: the making of guesses and modifying them in the light of our experience. We will tend to eliminate any reading which is not consistent with the situational clues.

You might like to try an exercise which tests Gombrich's view.

Exercise

Let's consider our position as a viewer looking at images, and how we project notional distances onto the fictive world of pictures. Look at the following:

After Goltzius, *Whale Washed Ashore in Holland* (*Art and Illusion*, illustration 55)

Claude Lorrain, *The Herdsman* (*Art and Illusion*, colour illustration III).

How would you estimate the notional distance of the viewer from the scene represented in illustration 55? Is this viewpoint nearer to, or further from, or at the same distance from the scene represented by Claude? Is it higher, lower, or at the same height?

Discussion

Two clues direct our reading, and since both images 'pass the test of consistency' discussed by Gombrich, we feel that we can 'trust' this reading for the whole of each picture. These two clues are, first, the scale of the human figures within each picture field and their relation to its borders, and, second, the horizon line in each image (recall the earlier discussion of the relationship of viewing point to horizon, pp.59–60).

The notional distance of the viewer from the scene represented in illustration 55, while not *very* remote (since the figures in the foreground are quite near to the lower and side borders of the picture field) is nevertheless greater than the notional distance of the viewer from the scene represented in Claude's painting. In the latter, the shepherd and his sheep occupy a much greater proportion of the picture surface than any comparably situated figure in illustration 55. Since we can be fairly certain that the shepherd in Claude's painting is not intended to be a giant, but a man of roughly the same size as the horseman in the view of the Whale, we perceive him as being nearer us than they are. The height of the horizon in illustration 55 suggests that our viewpoint is well above that of the foreground figures in that image, which explains our distance from them. The horizon line in illustration III is lower (don't be fooled by the mountains on the other side of the lake or river, their peaks are *above* the horizon line, which can be read as identical with the distant shoreline). It is only slightly higher than the sitting herdsman's viewpoint – the line of his eyes. If you measure the length of his torso and thighs, and estimate his standing height, you will find that his notional sightline very nearly coincides with the horizon. Imaginatively, we 'enter' the picture at almost the same height as the herdsman and very near him; a gentle climb to his vantage point, no more than a step or so, will enable us to share his solitary contemplation.

If we now turn away from this relatively narrow concern with the reading of spatial arrangements, we can see how our knowledge and experience might affect our broader responses to and interpretative 'guesses' about these paintings. It is hard to be sure from a colour reproduction, but the tonal range of colour in illustration III suggests a glowing sunset rather than a radiant sunrise. At any rate, colour and the disposition of lights and shadows combine to give an impression of some definite time at either end of the day. As we test the 'medley of forms and colours for coherent meaning', in Gombrich's phrase, this factor too will influence the meaning we project into the image. For example, if we are familiar with the old and widespread literary and theological conventions comparing the span of a day with a human lifespan, we may be inclined to lend some particular, perhaps melancholy, significance to the herdsman's 'meditative repose' – so different from the 'mindless browsing' of his cattle. Or we may recall yet another literary convention – invoked in Wordsworth's well-known, 'I wandered lonely as a cloud/That floats on high o'er vales and hills' – of the solitary poet's response to the countryside. Or we may project onto this painting some nostalgic thoughts about the 'idyllic' rural past, as opposed to the urban hurly-burly – an equally conventional response, already operating in antiquity and in the seventeenth century when Claude Lorrain painted such pictures as this for a mainly aristocratic clientèle. Our thoughts may equally well turn to a supposed harmony of man and nature, shattered by the Industrial Revolution, or of the joys and pleasures of a life of simple poverty. None of these associations is either a right or wrong response to or interpretation of this painting. What is important is that, whereas the perceptual clues of the panoramic view reproduced in illustration 55 suggest a distant, 'objective' reading which teaches the viewer something factual about the appearance of an unfamiliar animal (even if the artist got it wrong), Claude furnishes us with pictorial clues which encourage us to project onto this particular 'medley of forms and colours' a certain range of associations which assist us in the quest for meaning. Of course, no contemporary of the artist would have thought about the Industrial Revolution in front of this picture, since that series of events had not yet taken place. But many of our notions about industrialization are themselves determined by conventions – philosophical, literary and indeed pictorial – which long anticipate the factual circumstances of the eighteenth and nineteenth centuries. (Graham Martin has discussed pastoral conventions in literature in Units 4–6.) As long as these notions are current in Western culture, so paintings such as Claude's will continue to evoke a range of meanings analogous to those originally intended and experienced by the painter and his audience. Since the advent of photography has displaced engravings as instruments for transmitting factual information, the same is no longer true for images such as those in illustrations 54 and 55.

Gombrich suggests that once the spatial arrangements of illusionist art reached a peak of perfection, some artists rebelled by re-asserting the two-dimensional nature of paintings and thus the distinction between art and reality. This applies particularly to Cubism, which is discussed in sections XII, XIII and XIV of Chapter VIII. Instead of providing *consistent* clues for the beholder, Cubist artists provided contradictory hints of three-dimensional space, thus teasing the beholder and bringing his or her attention back to the flat picture plane, with all its tensions. The beholder's ability to project or 'make guesses' was thus pushed to its limits and the illusion sabotaged. Familiar objects (still lifes, portraits, landscapes) from familiar genres encourage the beholder to make guesses and to apply the test of consistency to Cubist images. The search for a consistent viewing from a single viewpoint is frustrated by the artist's studious, close scrutiny of objects simultaneously from various viewpoints and in alternative arrangements.

In Part Four Gombrich addresses the question of how art can advance, and, in particular, whether it is possible for the artist to see nature with an 'innocent eye', uninfluenced by knowledge, conventions or schemata.

Chapter IX, 'The analysis of vision in art'

It is difficult to seize the main thread of the argument of this chapter. Its main aim is to explode finally (if you still need convincing!) the 'myth' of the 'innocent eye', or the idea that artists can simply paint what they see, guided by pure observation of nature. Is it true, for example, that Turner painted what he *saw* rather than what he knew of the world? All representations, argues Gombrich, can be arranged along a scale extending from the schematic (the formulaic, the conventional) to the impressionist (where there are fewer schemata and a greater attempt to render impressions of the visible world more faithfully). However, he argues, artists like Ruskin – and the Impressionists – who claim that they see and portray nature with a totally innocent eye, are misguided. When they 'look' at nature they are *searching* for knowledge or meaning. Their expectations, guesses, and hypotheses influence what they see. Every observation is the result of a question we ask of nature. (This is as true of science as it is of art.) Artists must have a standard of comparison (perhaps the efforts of previous artists) before they can begin the process of making, matching and remaking. Artists produce coded *equivalents* to the real world, the 'illusion' or truth of which is to be judged by the internal *relationships* within a painting (between shapes, colours and sizes for example) rather than by a precise match between the object in reality and the way in which it is represented. In this effort they are invariably influenced by the work of their predecessors. Nevertheless, experimentation *can* lead an artist away from the 'prison of style' or the dominion of the schema. It is because artists can teach viewers to see the world in a new way that we can judge the success of their experiments and place them in relation to one another in a history of art. Section X illustrates this vividly through an analysis of Constable's art and that of his predecessors. If you wish to select only one section from this chapter, this is probably the most useful to you.

Chapter X, 'The experiment of caricature'

In this entertaining chapter Gombrich develops the idea, outlined in Chapter IX, that the invention of pictorial effects ('making', experimentation) is more powerful than the observation of nature, in the search for meaningful and convincing appearances in art. He looks particularly at the process of discovery and simplification in methods of rendering facial expression. The art of caricature is a splendid example of 'making' and experimentation in which artists are skilled in selecting those 'clues' which are important in order to meet the beholder half-way. Gombrich suggests that the skill of depicting facial expression owes more to an artist's manipulation of a visual language than to the desire to imitate reality. The schemata used by Le Brun and Hogarth are interesting examples of such a language. With artists like Daumier, the language of facial expression is used in a much looser, experimental way.

Chapter XI, 'From representation to expression'

This final chapter acts as a summary of Gombrich's previous arguments *and* attempts to extend them to other 'languages' of art. He has, so far, examined the language of representation as it relates to the way in which artists use forms and colours to represent the visible world. Now he turns to the language of *expression*: the way in which art uses forms and colours to express (or represent in the broadest sense of the term) the inner recesses of the mind. Why is it, for example, that we associate certain colours with certain moods or feelings? Gombrich concedes that, to a large extent, our responses to the expressive powers of art are intuitive. Nevertheless, expressive works of art are 'renderings within an acquired medium, a medium grown up through tradition and skill – that of the artist and that of the beholder'. As such, the equivalences between forms and colours on the one hand and feelings on the other are part of an acquired vocabulary. This applies equally to synaesthesia, the 'splashing over of the impression from one of our senses to the other' (for example, the equivalence between sensations of sight and sound in expressions such as 'loud colours'). When traditional associations between, say, certain colours and certain feelings become part of our vocabulary, we can narrow down the 'guesses' we make in interpreting the expressive significance of a work (we may, for example, 'read' red as angry or passionate). 'In our response to expression no less than in our reading of representation, our expectations of possibilities and probabilities must come into play' (p.316).

Gombrich extends this argument to the development of the personal style of an artist, which he likens to an accent in spoken language: an artist's personal style derives from the choices and vocabulary available to him or her. The fact that, in the past, these choices were often limited, should not be regarded as a disadvantage: familiarity and *controlled* innovation facilitated communication with the beholder. Paintings are not, then, simple, unmediated records, expressions or representations of an artist's feelings.

4 HOW GOMBRICH'S IDEAS IN *ART AND ILLUSION* RELATE TO UNITS 10–11

There are only three points to make here, but these should make clear how complementary Gombrich's text is to the approach taken in Units 10–11.

1 Broadly speaking, 'genre' is a kind of schema. By genre is meant here the categories based on subject-matter rather than the narrower sense of the 'depiction of everyday life'. The whole discussion of genre in the units exemplifies the operation of a particular form of schema, the conventional framework which the artist adopts and adapts. Because each of the different genres, at least within certain institutionalized frameworks, has particular conventions at any given point in time (for example, the 'brown grass' of Claude's landscapes, or the formal backgrounds of state portraiture), the notion of genre highlights Gombrich's central point that the practice of art and the viewing and interpretation of art hinges on a familiarity with the conventions of representation operative at a given time and place. It also focuses our attention on this aspect of the process of representation because both artist and viewer need to be familiar with a generic category. By extension, just as Gombrich's arguments on representation mean that representation needs to be seen to have a history, so the genres, as with all schemata, must depend on what has gone before in order to make sense.

2 An essential point in *Art and Illusion* is about constraints and limitations on representation. One type of constraint is imposed by the medium used by the artist (for example, oil, paint, pencil, charcoal), which determines to some extent what can be represented and how it can be done. This is a limitation that has been discussed in the preceding units, which concentrate on the possibilities of the medium and why pictures look as they do. Another point of focus in the units is on the possibilities and constraints determined by the function or intended purpose of an art object. This is taken up in the second part of the course.

3 Gombrich insists that representations have a history and that the requirements for and limitations upon representation are different in different historical periods. Gombrich makes points to this effect throughout the book, but the units you study in this course are more explicitly concerned with the social and cultural functions of art objects than is Gombrich.

These are general points which refer to the broad lines of enquiry which are common to Gombrich and your units. These points can be made more specific when you are looking at individual works of art by attending to the work and what it means in the following ways:

(a) *As a physical object.*

Note how the object has been made; a painting, for instance, may have been made of oil on canvas, or watercolour on paper, of a certain size and scale.

(b) *As a physical object in a context.*

Note that its original context and function may have been different from its present one (for example, as a devotional object on an altar rather than as a painting in an art gallery).

(c) *As a representation.*

Note how the artist has used certain devices and techniques (for example, lighting, viewpoint) to convince the spectator that the image is a plausible one; think about how meanings are constructed in the work by the treatment of subject-matter and the mode of representation used by the artist (remembering, of course, that not all works derive from a will to mimesis or resemblance: these are not the only criteria by which we judge art).

(d) *As a representation with a history.*

This incorporates the question of genre – the category or schema within which the work has been produced – and which changes historically. It follows that the meanings of a work of art relate back to previous works of art.

The main aim of the work you have been given over the last three weeks has been to emphasize the relationship between the subject-matter and function of a work of art and the kind of formal elements or visual conventions it uses. In the second part of the course there will be a greater emphasis on the relationship between works of art and the social context in which they were produced.

5 GOMBRICH'S IDEAS AND THE SECOND PART OF THE COURSE

Although *Art and Illusion* is not a text with an historical approach, its arguments about representation lend themselves fairly easily to a socio-historical approach, such as the one adopted in your interdisciplinary study. Indeed, the notion of representation is central to the interdisciplinary part of the course. The idea that an artwork (now in the sense of either a literary text or a work of visual art) is not a 'copy' or transcription of reality but a *re*-presentation involving the possibilities and constraints of a given medium (extend this now to the media of words or pictures) at a given time is crucial because the second part of the course is not just a survey of Victorian culture but a study of the relationship between Victorian culture and society.

You will find when you work on the second part of A102 that many of the ideas you have met in Gombrich have been assimilated into the approach adopted there. For instance, the idea of the 'beholder's share', the active part played by viewers, is re-framed in the discussions of paintings and texts: first, in what could be taken in the fairly Gombrichian sense of the currency of meanings and representations required by the spectator to make sense of an artwork, to interpret it as the Victorians did rather than the way we might with our very different 'mental set' today; secondly, in an extended sense of the spectator or viewer playing an active part as a consumer of art.

You might also bear in mind some of Gombrich's other key points as you read the second part of the course. Because different cultures have perceived the function of representation differently, you might consider how Victorian art fits into his view of 'making and matching' – for instance, the high degree of matching or correction in Victorian painting and its ideas of 'truth to nature'. Then, in the later part of the period you will study, Whistler's work shows the struggle *against* the schema of Victorian narrative painting. You may remember that Gombrich makes the point about the Victorian painting by William Frith, *Derby Day* (*Art and Illusion*, illustration 177; *Illustration booklet*, Plate 36), that it seems to leave nothing to the imagination. The emphasis, of course, is on the word 'seems' and Gombrich then goes on to show the part we play as viewers in interpreting the image as a plausible one. This vividly makes the point that all pictures leave something to the imagination however much they look otherwise, and the key question to ask is not just what they represent, but how.

Finally, Ruskin figures prominently later in A102 as both art critic and writer. Without anticipating this material, it would be appropriate to point out that Gombrich refers on several occasions to Ruskin's view of art. He refers to Ruskin's view of the 'innocent eye' (p.250 and p.260), the idea that art gets closer to nature (closer to the ideal of 'truth to nature') the less it relies on knowledge and convention. Gombrich's whole theory about the importance of conventions, indeed art as a conventional activity, was intended to challenge this still influential Ruskinian approach.

6 CONCLUSION: MEANING IN THE VISUAL ARTS

Meaning in the visual arts is as much a product of the viewer's 'effort after meaning', in Gombrich's phrase, as the artist's. For that reason, no work of art can ever have a definitive, constant and finite significance. Meaning will always depend on the *context* in which the viewer, as well as the work of art, is situated, and the 'equipment' which he or she brings to viewing. Part of that equipment is indeed biological, our ability to perceive colour and tonal relationships, etc. Part of it is culturally acquired but not usually conscious: reading a black-and-white drawing as a coded record of a full-coloured scene, not of a wire construction in the snow; a sculpted bust as a convention, not as a representation of a beheaded person; bringing a 'love of nature' to the appreciation of a landscape painting. But part of that equipment should also be a conscious knowledge of the historical possibilities, 'showing', as Gombrich writes, 'what a work of art cannot have meant within the framework of its style and situation', 'narrowing down the areas of misunderstanding'.

The 'situation' of a work of art is not, of course, only its immediate setting in its own time; it is also its place within the relatively autonomous realm of art. The framework of the genres is an important and obvious way in which works of art demonstrate their situation in that realm. Even before deciding on a motif, the artist can set out to paint 'a landscape', and will know that the artistic problems of the genre in Western art include first and foremost the representation of distance or space, and of light. Alternatively, still life tends to the scale of life and is concerned with the inter-relationship of volumes and shapes, and the way light is reflected from different kinds of surfaces. These are the 'givens' of both genres; these and similar considerations create a 'mental set' as much as style does, albeit in a rather different way.

Even today the academic hierarchy of the genres conditions the 'mental set' of artists, and if viewers are to narrow down the 'areas of misunderstanding' of the intended meanings, or probable meanings, or even appropriate meanings, of works of art they too must acquire a 'feel' for this system of classification. We have considered at some length the reactions of certain twentieth-century artists to public monumental genres (see in particular the discussion of Oldenburg's 'projected public monuments', pp.51–4). It seems clear that much of the popular mistrust of contemporary art is based on ignorance of this frame of reference. In other instances, generic hierarchies extend the range of meanings of works of art. Contemporary viewers of Tom Wesselmann's series of the *Great American Nude* (Colour plate 13) will probably pick up the references to poster art and the imagery of 'girlie' magazines. But the meaning of Wesselmann's pictures is enriched if we unscramble the generic mix of these paintings and assemblages. Their large size and the motif of the female nude recall that poetic branch of history painting sometimes called by its Italian name, *poesia* (see illustration 159 in *Art and Illusion*). Where Titian, and his fellow-Venetian, Giorgione, before him, set his nudes in landscape the better to recall ancient and Renaissance lyric poetry in which nymphs and shepherds dally in woods and copses, Wesselmann brutally reduces the Great American Nude to 'low' still life. Notice the constricted space and close viewpoint, the way erotic parts of the body, the mouth and breasts, are commingled, to the point of confusion, with fruit and inanimate, mass-produced objects. This is the nude, not of high poetry and the memory of classical nostalgia for a lost Golden Age, but a nude of today's age of gold, the exploitative consumer society. The poignancy of the brash image, a twentieth-century *vanitas,* may or may not have been intended by the artist, but it is a legitimate interpretation of the meaning of his work.

Even Wesselmann's wholly twentieth-century confections have their antecedents. Arcimboldo's punning image conflates still life with portraiture (Colour plate 14). You may wish to think out the possible meanings of this painting. A few verbal clues will help to 'narrow down areas of misunderstanding': Arcimboldo painted at the court of the Austrian Emperor Rudolf II, a famous collector; Vertumnus was an ancient Roman deity who protected orchards and gardens. And you might wish to consider what Gombrich says in the 'Retrospect' to *Art and Illusion:* 'The artist who wants to "represent" a real (or imagined) thing does not start by opening his eyes and looking about him but by taking colours and forms and building up the required image'.

It is hoped that you will now be in a position to embark more confidently on the search for meaning in a work of art. These units have suggested an approach to this task which incorporates a consideration of the following aspects of a work:

1 *Subject-matter or content.*

2 *Function (or purpose).* Is its job to tell a story, to act as an icon, to represent the visible world in some way?

3 *Provenance.* This term of art-historical jargon means, where has the work been? Who owned it, where was it originally placed? This is where the categories of *public* and *private* are so important. Tracing the various owners of the work after its creation can tell us a great deal, or reinforce what we may already suspect. A small-scale easel painting, for example, may have changed hands many times, since it is a 'commodity' like many others. A large funerary sculpture is more likely to have remained in its original setting, or to have entered a public collection directly from its original emplacement.

4 *Mode of representation or treatment of formal elements.* This also relates to the issue of *style.* Dating the work, relating it to other examples of its period style, will also tell us much about the choices available to the artist. *Scale* and *medium* are important here.

5 *The artist's intentions* – if these are known. Most of us will want to discover as much as we can about the artist's intentions, conscious or unconscious, and will look to both a work itself and to other contingent evidence in order to elucidate them. The meanings we derive from a painting are not, of course, limited to those intended by the artist.

6 *Genre* (relates to 1 above). This can tell us much about the status of a work of art at the time of its making and of the traditional frameworks within which artists worked.

7 The *conventions* and *traditions* of art known to an artist and his/her public relate to 1, 4, 5 and 6 above and can help us to understand the meaning of a work of art.

8 *Circumstances of production.* What are the likely circumstances of production? How, when, under what conditions was the work made? A large bronze sculpture, for example, will always argue for a commission, great expense, a high degree of technological know-how, specialist collaboration, a foundry, etc. A small drawing, in contrast, suggests more rapid and individual production (although it argues for the availability of ready-made paper), and does not necessarily (is indeed unlikely to) imply a patron and commission for the drawing itself. Dating a work may be seen to be a part of the circumstances

of its production. All of these factors (including the possible wishes of a patron) can tell us about the status and significance of a work.

9 *Socio-historical context* of the work and of its beholder(s). This can tell us about the cultural value systems surrounding the production and reception of a work. An art historian may wish, after discussing the original intended significance of a work of art, also to draw attention to the meanings which have accreted to the work since its creation – its 'after-life'. For example, the significance of Raphael's Madonnas has undergone many changes. From choice collector's pieces, they became canonic works – that is, setting a standard by which other works of art were judged, and to which other artists aspired (even in the Victorian period, as is demonstrated in Television programme 21 *Victorian Views of the Art of the Past).* They are seen as a chocolate-box cliché by many of our contemporaries who have different moral, social, commercial and political priorities.

All of the above aspects are, of course, inter-related. The answers to many of the questions listed will not be available, or not available with the same degree of precision. Nevertheless, since they are interdependent, the questions should all be raised. 'Educated guesses', based on one's understanding of the context, may provide a clue to subsequent answers. The detective work involved may help to explain, at the very least, why your own responses to a painting can differ from those it elicited at the time of its making. To a twentieth-century viewer unacquainted with the art of the past the costumes of the figures in West's *Death of General Wolfe* (Colour Plate 8) might appear perfectly appropriate and the General's pose and expression somewhat melodramatic. The interpretation given by an eighteenth-century viewer accustomed to classical dress in history paintings, to representations of the dying Christ and to the stereotypes of facial expression codified by Le Brun, would have been quite different.

REFERENCES FOR UNITS 10-12

A. Cole (1992) *Perspective,* Dorling Kindersley in association with National Gallery Publications, London.

W. Friedlander (1955) *Caravaggio Studies,* Princeton University Press.

E.H. Gombrich (1966) *Norm and Form,* Phaidon.

E.H. Gombrich (1977, 5th edn.) *Art and Illusion,* Phaidon (first published 1960) (Set Book).

E.H. Gombrich (1985, 14th edn.) *The Story of Art,* Phaidon (first published 1950).

N. Hilliard, *Arte of Limning;* reprinted by the Walpole Society, 1912, Vol. 1.

R. Hughes (1980) *The Shock of the New,* Thames and Hudson.

E. Lucie-Smith (1984) *Dictionary of Art Terms*, Thames and Hudson.

C. Oldenburg in Arts Council of Great Britain (1970) *Claes Oldenburg,* exhibition catalogue.

The Open University (1986) A353 *Art in Fifteenth-Century Italy.*

The Open University (1993) A206 *The Enlightenment.*

Ovid, *Metamorphoses,* Book I; prose translation by F.J. Miller, Loeb Classical Library, 1966.

M. Pointon (1993) *Hanging the Head*, Yale University Press.

Herbert Read (1964, reprinted 1992), *Modern Sculpture: a concise history,* Thames and Hudson.

Sir J. Reynolds, *Discourses on Art*, edited by R.R. Wark, Yale University Press, 1975.

C. Wood (1988) *The Pre-Raphaelites*, Weidenfeld and Nicolson.

F. Woolf and M. Cassin (1987) *Bodylines: The Human Figure in Art,* The National Gallery, London.